THE DAY OF DAYS

LOUIS JOSEPH VANCE

1st WORLD
LIBRARY
Literary Society

The Day of Days

Louis Joseph Vance

© 1st World Library, 2006
PO Box 2211
Fairfield, IA 52556
www.1stworldlibrary.com
First Edition

LCCN: 2006935244

Softcover ISBN: 1-4218-2497-3
Hardcover ISBN: 1-4218-2397-7
eBook ISBN: 1-4218-2597-X

Purchase *"The Day of Days"*
as a traditional bound book at:
www.1stWorldLibrary.com/purchase.asp?ISBN=1-4218-2497-3

1st World Library is a literary, educational organization
dedicated to:

- Creating a free internet library of downloadable ebooks

- Hosting writing competitions and offering book
publishing scholarships.

Interested in more 1st World Library books?
contact: literacy@1stworldlibrary.com
Check us out at: www.1stworldlibrary.com

1ˢᵗ World Library Literary Society

Giving Back to the World

"If you want to work on the core problem, it's early school literacy."

- James Barksdale, former CEO of Netscape

"No skill is more crucial to the future of a child, or to a democratic and prosperous society, than literacy."

- Los Angeles Times

Literacy... means far more than learning how to read and write... The aim is to transmit... knowledge and promote social participation."

- UNESCO

"Literacy is not a luxury, it is a right and a responsibility. If our world is to meet the challenges of the twenty-first century we must harness the energy and creativity of all our citizens."

- President Bill Clinton

"Parents should be encouraged to read to their children, and teachers should be equipped with all available techniques for teaching literacy, so the varying needs and capacities of individual kids can be taken into account."

- Hugh Mackay

CONTENTS

I

THE DUB

"Smell," P. Sybarite mused aloud....

For an instant he was silent in depression. Then with extraordinary vehemence he continued crescendo: "Stupid-stagnant-sepulchral-sempiternally-sticky-Smell!"

He paused for both breath and words—pondered with bended head, knitting his brows forbiddingly.

"Supremely squalid, sinisterly sebaceous, sombrely sociable Smell " he pursued violently.

Momentarily his countenance cleared; but his smile was as fugitive asthe favour of princes.

Vindictively champing the end of a cedar penholder, he groped for expression: "Stygian ... sickening ... surfeiting ... slovenly ... sour...."

He shook his head impatiently and clawed the impregnated atmosphere with a tragic hand.

"*Stench!*" he perorated in a voice tremulous with emotion.

Even that comprehensive monosyllable was far from satisfactory.

"Oh, what's the use?" P. Sybarite despaired.

Alliteration could no more; his mother-tongue itself seemed poverty-stricken, his native wit inadequate. With decent meekness he owned himself unfit for the task to which he had set himself.

"I'm only a dub," he groaned—" a poor, God-forsaken, prematurely aged and indigent dub!"

For ten interminable years the aspiration to do justice to the Genius of the Place had smouldered in his humble bosom; to-day for the first time he had attempted to formulate a meet apostrophe to that God of his Forlorn Destiny; and now he chewed the bitter cud of realisation that all his eloquence had proved hopelessly poor and lame and halting.

Perched on the polished seat of a very tall stool, his slender legs fraternising with its legs in apparently inextricable intimacy; sharp elbows digging into the nicked and ink-stained bed of a counting-house desk; chin some six inches above the pages of a huge leather-covered ledger, hair rumpled and fretful, mouth doleful, eyes disconsolate—he gloomed...

On this the eve of his thirty-second birthday and likewise the tenth anniversary of his servitude, the appearance of P. Sybarite was elaborately normal—varying, as it did, but slightly from one year's-end to the other.

His occupation had fitted his head and shoulders with a deceptive but none the less perennial stoop. His means had endowed him with a single outworn suit of ready-made clothing which, shrinking sensitively on each successive application of the tailor's sizzling goose, had come to disclose his person with disconcerting candour—sleeves too short, trousers at once too short and too narrow, waistcoat buttons straining over his chest, coat buttons refusing to recognise a buttonhole save that at the waist. Circumstances these that added measurably to his apparent age, lending him the semblance of maturity attained while still in the shell of youth.

The ruddy brown hair thatching his well-modelled head, his sanguine colouring, friendly blue eyes and mobile lips suggested Irish lineage; and his hands which, though thin and clouded with smears of ink, were strong and graceful (like the slender feet in his shabby shoes) bore out the suggestion with an added hint of gentle blood.

But whatever his antecedents, the fact is indisputable that P. Sybarite, just then, was most miserable, and not without cause; for the Genius of the Place held his soul in Its melancholy bondage.

The Place was the counting-room in the warehouse of Messrs. Whigham & Wimper, *Hides & Skins*; and the Genius of it was the reek of hides both raw and dressed—an effluvium incomparable, a passionate individualist of an odour, as rich as the imagination of an editor of Sunday supplements, as rare as a reticent author, as friendly as a stray puppy.

For ten endless years the body and soul of P. Sybarite had been thrall to that Smell; for a complete decade he had inhaled it continuously nine hours each day, six days each week—and had felt lonesome without it on every seventh day.

But to-day all his being was in revolt, bitterly, hopelessly mutinous against this evil and overbearing Genius....

The warehouse—impregnable lair of the Smell, from which it leered smug defiance at the sea-sweet atmosphere of the lower city—occupied a walled-in arch of the Brooklyn Bridge, fronting on Frankfort Street, in that part of Town still known to elder inhabitants as "the Swamp." Above rumbled the everlasting inter-borough traffic; to the right, on rising ground, were haunts of roaring type-mills grinding an endless grist of news; to the left, through a sudden dip and down a long decline, a world of sober-sided warehouses, degenerating into slums, circumscribed by sleepy South Street; all, this afternoon, warm and languorous in the lazy breeze of a sunny April Saturday.

The counting-room was a cubicle contrived by enclosing a corner of the ground-floor with two walls and a ceiling of match-boarding. Into this constricted space were huddled two imposing roll-top desks, P. Sybarite's high counter, and the small flat desk of the shipping clerk, with an iron safe, a Remington typewriter, a copy-press, sundry chairs and spittoons, a small gas-heater, and many tottering columns of dusty letter-files. The window-panes, encrusted with perennial deposits of Atmosphere, were less transparent than translucent, and so little the latter that electric bulbs burned all day long whenever the skies were overcast. Also, the windows were fixed and set against the outer air—impregnable to any form of assault less impulsive than a stone cast by an irresponsible hand. A door, set craftily in the most inconvenient spot imaginable, afforded both ventilation and access to an aisle which led tortuously between bales of hides to doors opening upon a waist-high stage, where trucks backed up to receive and to deliver.

Immured in this retreat, P. Sybarite was very much shut away from all joy of living—alone with his job (which at present nothing pressed) with Giant Despair and its interlocutor Ennui, and with that blatant, brutish, implacable Smell of Smells....

To all of these, abruptly and with ceremony, Mr. George Bross, shipping clerk, introduced himself: a brawny young man in shirt-sleeves, wearing a visorless cap of soiled linen, an apron of striped ticking, pencils behind both angular red ears, and a smudge of marking-ink together with a broad irritating smile upon a clownish countenance.

Although in receipt of a smaller wage than P. Sybarite (who earned fifteen dollars per week) George squandered fifteen cents on newspapers every Sunday morning for sheer delight in the illuminated "funny sheets."

In one hand he held an envelope.

Draping himself elegantly over Mr. Wimper's desk, George regarded P. Sybarite with an indulgent and compassionate smile and wagged a doggish head at him. From these symptoms inferring that his fellow-employee was in the throes of a witticism, P. Sybarite cocked an apprehensive eye and tightened his thin-lipped, sensitive mouth.

"O you—!" said George; and checked to enjoy a rude giggle.

At this particular moment a mind-reader would have been justified in regarding P. Sybarite with suspicion. But beyond taking the pen from between his teeth he didn't move; and he said nothing at all.

The shipping clerk presently controlled his mirth sufficiently to permit unctuous enunciation of the following cryptic exclamation:

"O you Perceval!"

P. Sybarite turned pale.

"You little rascal!" continued George, brandishing the envelope. "You've been cunning, you have; but I've found you out at last.... *Per*-ce-val!"

Over the cheeks of P. Sybarite crept a delicate tint of pink. His eyes wavered and fell. He looked, and was, acutely unhappy.

"You're a sly one, you are," George gloated—"always signin' your name 'P. Sybarite' and pretendin' your maiden monaker was 'Peter'! But now we know you! Take off them whiskers— Perceval!"

A really wise mind-reader would have called a policeman, then and there; for mayhem was the least of the crimes contemplated by P. Sybarite. But restraining himself, he did nothing more than disentangle his legs, slip down from the tall stool, and approach Mr. Bross with an outstretched hand.

"If that letter's for me," he said quietly, "give it here, please."

"Special d'liv'ry—just come," announced George, holding the letter high, out of easy reach, while he read in exultant accents the traitorous address: "'Perceval Sybarite, Esquire, Care of Messrs. Whigham and Wimper'! O you Perceval—Esquire!"

"Give me my letter," P. Sybarite insisted without raising his voice.

"Gawd knows *I* don't want it," protested George. "I got no truck with your swell friends what know your real name and write to you on per-*fumed* paper with monograms and everything."

He held the envelope close to his nose and sniffed in ecstasy until it was torn rudely from his grasp.

"Here!" he cried resentfully. "Where's your manners?... Perceval!"

Dumb with impotent rage, P. Sybarite climbed back on his stool, while George sat down at his desk, lighted a Sweet Caporal (it was after three o'clock and both the partners were gone for the day) and with a leer watched the bookkeeper carefully slit the envelope and withdraw its enclosures.

Ignoring him, P. Sybarite ran his eye through the few lines of notably careless feminine handwriting:

MY DEAR PERCEVAL,—

Mother & I had planned to take some friends to the theatre to-night and bought a box for the Knickerbocker several weeks ago, but now we have decided to go to Mrs. Hadley-Owen's post-Lenten masquerade ball instead, and as none of our friends can use the tickets, I thought possibly you might like them. They say Otis Skinner is *wonderful*. Of course you may not care to sit in a stage box without a dress suit, but perhaps you won't mind. If you do, maybe you know somebody else who could go properly dressed.

Your aff'te cousin,

MAE ALYS.

The colour deepened in P. Sybarite's cheeks, and instantaneous pin-pricks of fire enlivened his long-suffering eyes. But again he said nothing. And since his eyes were downcast, George was unaware of their fitful incandescence.

Puffing vigorously at his cigarette, he rocked back and forth on the hind legs of his chair and crowed in jubilation: "Perceval! O you great, big, beautiful Perc'!"

P. Sybarite made a motion as if to tear the note across, hesitated, and reconsidered. Through a long minute he sat thoughtfully examining the tickets presented him by his aff'te cousin.

In his ears rang the hideous tumult of George's joy:

"*Per-ce-val!*"

Drawing to him one of the Whigham & Wimper letterheads, P. Sybarite dipped a pen, considered briefly, and wrote rapidly and freely in a minute hand:

MY DEAR MAE ALYS:—

Every man has his price. You know mine. Pocketing false pride, I accept your bounty with all the gratitude and humility becoming in a poor relation. And if arrested for appearing in the box without evening clothes, I promise solemnly to brazen it out, pretend that I bought the tickets myself—or stole them—and keep the newspapers ignorant of our kinship. Fear not—trust me—and enjoy the masque as much as I mean to enjoy "Kismet."

And if you would do me the greatest of favours—should you ever again find an excuse to write me on any matter, please address me by the initial of my ridiculous first name only; it is of course impossible for me to live down the deep damnation of having been born a Sybarite; but the indulgence of my friends can save me the further degradation of being known as Perceval.

With thanks renewed and profound, I remain, all things considered,

Remotely yours,

P. SYBARITE.

This he sealed and addressed in a stamped envelope: then thrust his pen into a raw but none the less antique potato; covered the red and black inkwells; closed the ledger; locked the petty-cash box and put it away; painstakingly arranged the blotters, paste-pot, and all the clerical paraphernalia of his desk; and slewed round on his stool to blink pensively at Mr. Bross.

That gentleman, having some time since despaired of any response to his persistent baiting, was now preoccupied with a hand-mirror and endeavours to erase the smudge of marking-ink from his face by means of a handkerchief which he now and again moistened in an engagingly natural and unaffected manner.

"It's no use, George," observed P. Sybarite presently. "If you're in earnest in these public-spirited endeavours to—how would you put it?—to remove the soil from your map, take a tip from an old hand and go to soap and water. I know it's painful, but, believe me, it's the only way."

George looked up in some surprise.

"Why, *there* you are, little Bright Eyes!" he exclaimed with spirit. "I was beginnin' to be afraid this sittin' would pass off without a visit from Uncle George's pet control. Had little Perceval any message from the Other Side th'safternoon?"

"One or two," assented P. Sybarite gravely. "To begin with, I'm going to shut up shop in just five minutes; and if you don't want to show yourself on the street looking like a difference of opinion between a bull-calf and a fountain pen—"

"Gotcha," interrupted George, rising and putting away hand-kerchief and mirror. "I'll drown myself, if you say so. Anythin's better'n letting you talk me to death."

"One thing more."

Splashing vigorously at the stationary wash-stand, George looked gloomily over his shoulder, and in sepulchral accents uttered the one word:

"Shoot!"

"How would you like to go to the theatre to-night?"

George soaped noisily his huge red hands.

"I'd like it so hard," he replied, "that I'm already dated up for an evenin' of intellect'al enjoyment. Me and Sammy Holt 'a goin' round to Miner's Eight' Avenoo and bust up the show. You can trail if you wanta, but don't blame me if some big, coarse, two-fisted guy hears me call you Perceval and picks on you."

He bent forward over the bowl, and the cubicle echoed with sounds of splashing broken by gasps, splutters, and gurgles, until he straightened up, groped blindly for two yards or so of dark grey roller-towel ornamenting the adjacent wall, buried his face in its hospitable obscurity, and presently emerged to daylight with a countenance bright and shining above his chin, below his eyebrows, and in front of his ears.

"How's that?" he demanded explosively. "Come off all right—didn't it?"

P. Sybarite inclined his head to one side and regarded the outcome of a reform administration.

"You look almost naked around the nose," he remarked at length. "But you'll do. Don't worry.... When I asked if you'd like to go to the theatre to-night, I meant it—and I meant a regular show, at a Broadway house."

"Quit your kiddin'," countered Mr. Bross indulgently. "Come along: I got an engagement to walk home and save a nickel, and so've you."

"Wait a minute," insisted P. Sybarite, without moving. "I'm in earnest about this. I offer you a seat in a stage-box at the Knickerbocker Theatre to-night, to see Otis Skinner in 'Kismet.'"

George's eyes opened simultaneously with his mouth.

"Me?" he gasped. "Alone?"

P. Sybarite shook his head. "One of a party of four."

"Who else?" George demanded with pardonable caution.

"Miss Prim, Miss Leasing, myself."

Removing his apron of ticking, the shipping clerk opened a drawer in his desk, took put a pair of cuffs, and begun to adjust them to the wristbands of his shirt.

"Since when did you begin to snuff coke?" he enquired with

mild compassion.

"I'm not joking." P. Sybarite displayed the tickets. "A friend sent me these. I'll make up the party for to-night as I said, and let you come along—on one condition."

"Go to it."

"You must promise me to quit calling me Perceval, here or any place else, to-day and forever!"

George chuckled; paused; frowned; regarded P. Sybarite with narrow suspicion.

"And never tell anybody, either," added the other, in deadly earnest.

George hesitated.

"Well, it's your *name*, ain't it?" he grumbled.

"That's not my fault. I'll be damned if I'll be called Perceval."

"And what if I keep on?"

"Then I'll make up my theatre party without you—and break your neck into the bargain," said P. Sybarite intensely.

"You?" George laughed derisively. "You break *my* neck? Can the comedy, beau. Why, I could eat you alive, Perceval."

P. Sybarite got down from his stool. His face was almost colourless, but for two bright red spots, the size of quarters, beneath either cheek-bone. He was half a head shorter than the shipping clerk, and apparently about half as wide; but there was sincerity in his manner and an ominous snap in the unflinching stare of his blue eyes.

"Please yourself," he said quietly. "Only—don't say I didn't warn you!"

"Ah-h!" sneered George, truculent in his amazement. "What's eatin' you?"

"We're going to settle this question before you leave this warehouse. I won't be called Perceval by you or any other pink-eared cross between Balaam's ass and a laughing hyena."

Mr. Bross gaped with resentment, which gradually overcame his better judgment.

"You won't, eh?" he said stridently. "I'd like to know what you're going to do to stop me, Perce—"

P. Sybarite stepped quickly toward him and George, with a growl, threw out his hands in a manner based upon a somewhat hazy conception of the formulae of self-defence. To his surprise, the open hand of the smaller man slipped swiftly past what he called his "guard" and placed a smart, stinging slap upon lips open to utter the syllable "val."

Bearing with indignation, he swung his right fist heavily for the head of P. Sybarite. Somehow, strangely, it missed its goal and ...

George Bross sat upon the dusty, grimy floor, batted his eyes, ruefully rubbed the back of his head, and marvelled at the reverberations inside it.

Then he became conscious of P. Sybarite some three feet distant, regarding him with tight-lipped interest.

"Good God!" George ejaculated with feeling. "Did *you* do that to me?"

"I did," returned P. Sybarite curtly. "Want me to prove it?"

"Plenty, thanks," returned the shipping clerk morosely, as he picked himself up and dusted off his clothing. "Gee! You got a wallop like the kick of a mule, Per—"

"Cut that!"

"P.S., I mean," George amended hastily. "Why didn't you ever tell me you was Jeffries's sparrin' partner?"

"I'm not and never was, and furthermore I didn't hit you," replied P. Sybarite. "All I did was to let you fall over my foot and bump your head on the floor. You're a clumsy brute, you know, George, and if you tried it another time you *might* dent that dome of yours. Better accept my offer and be friends."

"Never call you Per—"

"Don't say it!"

"Oh, all right—all right," George agreed plaintively. "And if I promise, I'm in on that theatre party?"

"That's my offer."

"It's hard," George sighed regretfully—"damn' hard. But whatever *you* say goes. I'll keep your secret."

"Good!" P. Sybarite extended one of his small, delicately modelled hands. "Shake," said he, smiling wistfully.

II

INSPIRATION

When they had locked in the Genius of the Place to batten upon itself until seven o'clock Monday morning, P. Sybarite and Mr. Bross, with at least every outward semblance of complete amity, threaded the roaring congestion in narrow-chested Frankfort Street, boldly breasted the flood tide of homing Brooklynites, won their way through City Hall Park, and were presently swinging shoulder to shoulder up the sunny side of lower Broadway.

To be precise, the swinging stride was practised only by Mr. Bross; P. Sybarite, instinctively aware that any such mode of locomotion would ill become one of his inches, contented himself with keeping up—his gait an apparently effortless, tireless, and comfortable amble, congruent with bowed shoulders, bended head, introspective eyes, and his aspect in general of patient preoccupation.

From time to time George, who was maintaining an unnatural and painful silence, his mental processes stagnant with wonder and dull resentment, eyed his companion askance, with furtive suspicion. Their association was now one of some seven years' standing; and it seemed a grievous thing that, after posing so long as the patient butt of his rude humour, P.S. should have so suddenly turned and proved himself the better man—and that not mentally alone.

"Lis'n—" George interjected of a sudden.

P. Sybarite started. "Eh?" he enquired blankly.

"I wanna know where you picked up all that classy footwork."

"Oh," returned P.S., depreciatory, "I used to spar a bit with the fellows when I was a—ah—when I was younger."

"When you was at *what*?" insisted Bross, declining to be fobbed off with any such flimsy evasion.

"When I was at liberty to."

"Huh! You mean, when you was at college."

"Please yourself," said P. Sybarite wearily.

"Well, you was at college oncet, wasn't you?"

"I was," P.S. admitted with reluctance; "but I never graduated. When I was twenty-one I had to quit to go to work for Whigham & Wimper."

"G'wan," commented the other. "They ain't been in business twenty-five years."

"I'm only thirty-one."

"More news for Sweeny. You'll never see forty again."

"That statement," said P. Sybarite with some asperity, "is an uncivil untruth dictated by a spirit of gratuitous conten-tiousness—"

"Good God!" cried Bross in alarm. "I'm wrong and you're right and I won't do it again—and forgive me for livin'!"

"With pleasure," agreed P. Sybarite pleasantly....

"It's a funny world," George resumed in philosophic humour, after a time. "You wouldn't think I could work in the same dump with you seven years and only be startin' to find out things about you—like to-day. I always thought your name was Pete—honest."

"Continue to think so," P. Sybarite advised briefly.

"Your people had money, didn't they, oncet?"

"I've been told so, but if true, it only goes to prove there's nothing in the theory of heredity...."

"I gotcha," announced Bross, upon prolonged and painful analysis.

"How?" asked P. Sybarite, who had fallen to thinking of other matters.

"I mean, I just dropped to your high-sign to mind my own business. All right, P.S. Far be it from me to wanta pry into your Past. Besides, I'm scared to—never can tell what I'll turn up—like, f'rinstance, Per—"

"Steady!"

"Like that they usta call you when you was innocent, I mean."

To this P. Sybarite made no response; and George subsided into morose reflections. It irked him sore to remember he had been worsted by the meek little slip of a bookkeeper trotting so quietly at his elbow.

He was a man of his word, was George Bross; not for anything would he have gone back on his promise to keep secret that afternoon's titillating discovery; likewise he was a covetous soul, loath to forfeit the promised treat; withal he was human (after his kind) and since reprisals were not barred by their understanding, he began then and there to ponder the same.

One way or another, that day's humiliation must be balanced; else he might never again hold up his head in the company of gentlemen of spirit.

But how to compass this desire, frankly puzzled him. It were cowardly to contemplate knockin' the block off'n P. Sybarite; the disparity of their statures forebade; moreover, George entertained a vexatious suspicion that P. Sybarite's explanation on his recent downfall had not been altogether disingenuous; he didn't quite believe it had been due solely to his own clumsiness and an adventitious foot.

"That sort of thing don't never *happen*," George assured himself privately. "I was outclassed, all right, all right. What I wanna know is: where'd he couple up with the ring-wisdom?"

Repeated if covert glances at his companion supplied no clue; P. Sybarite's face remained as uncommunicative as well-to-do relations by marriage; his shadowy, pale and wistful smile denoted, if anything, only an almost childlike pleasure in anticipation of the evening's promised amusement.

Suddenly it was borne in upon the shipping clerk that in the probable arrangement of the proposed party he would be expected to dance attendance upon Miss Violet Prim, leaving P. Sybarite free to devote himself to Miss Lessing. Whereupon George scowled darkly.

"P.S.'s got his nerve with him," he protested privately, "to cop out the one pippin in the house all for his lonely. It's a wonder he wouldn't slip her a chanct to enjoy herself with summon' her own age...."

"Not," he admitted ruefully, "that I'd find it healthy to pull any rough stuff with Vi lookin' on. I don't even like to think of myself lampin' any other skirt while Violet's got *her* wicks trimmed and burnin' bright."

Then he made an end to envy for the time being, and turned

his attention to more pressing concerns; but though he pondered with all his might and main, it seemed impossible to excogitate any way to square his account with P. Sybarite. And when, at Thirty-eighth Street, the latter made an excuse to part with George, instead of going home in his company, the shipping clerk was too thoroughly disgusted to question the subterfuge. He was, indeed, a bit relieved; the temporary dissociation promised just so much more time for solitary conspiracy.

Turning west, he was presently prompted by that arch-comedian Destiny (disguised as Thirst) to drop into Clancey's for a shell of beer.

Now in Clancey's George found a crumpled copy of the *Evening Journal* almost afloat on the high-tide of the dregs-drenched bar. Rescuing the sheet, he smoothed it out, examined (grinning) its daily meed of comics, read every word on the "Sports Page," ploughed through the weekly vaudeville charts, scanned the advertisements, and at length reviewed the news columns with a listless eye.

It may have been the stimulation of his drink, but it was probably nothing more nor less than jealousy that sparked his sluggish imagination as he contemplated a two-column reproduction in coarse half-tone of a photograph entitled "Marian Blessington." Slowly the light dawned upon mental darkness; slowly his grin broadened and became fixed—even as his great scheme for the confusion and confounding of P. Sybarite took shape and matured.

He left Clancey's presently, stepping high, with a mind elate; foretasting victory; convinced that he harboured within him the makings of a devil of a fellow, all the essential quali-fications of (not to put *too* fine a point upon it) a regular wag....

III

THE GLOVE COUNTER

With a feeling of some guilt, becoming in one who stoops to unworthy artifice, P. Sybarite walked slowly on up Broadway a little way, then doubled on his trail, going softly until a swift and stealthy survey westward from the corner of Thirty-eighth Street assured him that George was not skulking thereabouts to spy upon him. Then mending his pace, he held briskly on toward the shopping district.

From afar the clock recently restored to its coign high above unlovely Greeley Square warned him that his hour was fleeting: in twenty minutes it would be six o'clock; at six, sharp, Blessington's would close its doors. Distressed, he scurried on, crossed Thirty-fourth Street, aimed himself courageously for the wide entrance of the department store, battled manfully through the retreating army of feminine shoppers—and gained the glove counter with a good fifteen minutes to spare.

And there he halted, confused and blushing in recognition of circumstances as unpropitious as unforeseen.

These consisted in three girls behind the counter and one customer before it; the latter commanding the attention and services of a fair young woman with a pleasant manner; while of the two disengaged saleswomen, one bold, disdainful brunette was preoccupied with her back hair and prepared mutinously to ignore anything remotely resembling a belated customer whose demands might busy her beyond the closing hour, and the other had a merry eye and a receptive smile for the hesitant little man with the funny clothes and the quaint pink face of embarrassment. In most abject consternation, P. Sybarite turned and fled.

Weathering the end of the glove counter and shaping a course through the aisle that paralleled it, he found himself in a channel of horrors, threatened on one side by a display of most intimate lingerie, belaced and beribboned distractingly, on the other by a long rank of slender and gracious (if stolid) feminine limbs, one and all neatly amputated above their bended knees and bedight in silken hosiery to shame the rainbow; while to right and left, behind these impudent revelations, lurked sirens with shameless eyes and mouths of scarlet mockery.

A cold sweat damped the forehead of P. Sybarite. Inconsistently, his face flamed. He stared fixedly dead ahead and tore through that aisle like a delicate-minded jack-rabbit. He thought giggles were audible in his wake; and ere he could escape found his way barred by Authority and Dignity in one wonderfully frock-coated person.

"You were looking for something?" demanded this menace incarnate, in an awful voice accompanied by a terrible gesture.

P. Sybarite brought up standing, his nose six inches from and his eyes held in fascination to the imitation pearl scarf-pin in the beautiful cravat affected by his interlocutor.

"Gloves—!" he gasped guiltily.

"This way, if you please."

With this, Dignity and Authority clamped an inexorable hand about his upper arm, swung him round, and piloted him gently but ruthlessly back the way he had come, back to the glove counter, where he was planted directly in front of the dashing, dark saleslady with absorbing back hair and the manner of remote hauteur.

"Miss Brady, this gentleman wants to see some gloves."

The eyes of Miss Brady flashed ominously; as plain as print, they said: "Does, does he? Well, leave him to *me*!"

Aloud, she murmured from an incalculable distance: "Oh, very well!"

A moment later, looking over the customer's head, she added icily: "What kind?"

The floor-walker retired, leaving P. Sybarite a free agent but none the less haunted by a feeling that a suspicious eye was being kept on the small of his back. He stammered something quite inarticulate.

The brune goddess shaped ironic lips:

"Chauffeurs', I presoom?"

A measure of self-possession—akin to the deadly coolness of the cornered rat—returned to the badgered little man.

"No," he said evenly—"ladies', if you please."

Scornfully Miss Brady impaled the back of her head with a lead pencil.

"Other end of the counter, please," she announced. "I don't handle ladies' gloves!"

"I'm sure of that," returned P. Sybarite meekly; left her standing; and presented himself for the inspection of the fair young woman with the pleasant manner, who was now free of her late customer.

She recognised him with surprise, but none the less with a friendly smile.

"Why, Mr. Sybarite—!"

In his hearing, her voice was rarest music. He gulped; stammered "Miss Lessing!" and was stricken dumb by perception of his effrontery.

"Can I do anything for you?"

He breathed in panic: "Gloves—"

"For a lady, Mr. Sybarite?"

He nodded as expressively as any automaton.

"What kind?"

"I—I don't know."

"For day or evening wear?"

He wagged a dismal head: "I don't know."

Amusement touched her eyes and lips so charmingly that he thought of the sea at dawn, rimpled by the morning breeze, gay with the laughter of young sunlight.

"Surely you must!" she insisted.

"No," he contended in stubborn melancholy.

"Oh, I see. You wish to make a present—?"

"I—ah—suppose so," he admitted under pressure—"yes."

"Evening gloves are always acceptable. Does she go often to the theatre?"

"I—don't know."

The least suspicion of perplexed frown knitted the eyebrows of Miss Lessing.

"Well ... is she old or young?"

"I—ah—couldn't say."

"Mr. Sybarite!" said the young woman with decision.

He fixed an apprehensive gaze to hers—which inclined to disapproval, if with reservations.

"Yes, Miss Lessing?"

"Do you really want to buy gloves?"

"No-o...."

"Then what under the sun *do* you want?"

He noticed suddenly that, however impatient her tone, her eyes were still kindly. Eyes of luminous hazel brown they were, wide open and clear beneath dark and delicate brows; eyes that assorted oddly with her hair of pale, dull gold, rendering her prettiness both individual and distinctive.

Somehow he found himself more at ease.

"Please," he begged humbly, "show me some gloves—any kind—it doesn't matter—and pretend you believe I want to buy 'em. I don't really. I—I only want—ah—word with you before you go home."

If this were impertinence, the girl elected quickly not to resent it. She turned to the shelves behind her, took down a box or two, and opened them for his inspection.

"These are very nice," she suggested quietly.

"I think so, too." He grinned uneasily. "What I want to say is—will you be my guest at the theatre to-night?"

"I'm afraid I don't understand you," she said, replacing the gloves.

"With Miss Prim and George Bross," he amended hastily. "Somebody—a friend—sent me a box for 'Kismet.' I thought—possibly—you might care to go. It—it would give me great pleasure."

Miss Lessing held up another pair of gloves.

"These are three-fifty-nine," she said absently. "Why did you come here to ask me?"

"I—I was afraid you might make some other engagement for the evening."

He couldn't have served his cause more handsomely than by uttering just that transparent evasion. In a thought she understood: at their boarding-house he could have found no ready opportunity to ask her save in the presence of others; and he was desperately afraid of a refusal.

After all, he had reason to be: they were only table acquaintances of a few weeks' standing. It was most presumptuous of him to dream that she would accept....

On the other hand, he was (she considered gravely) a decent, manly little body, and had shown her more civility and deference than all the rest of the boarding-house and shop people put together. And she rather liked him and was reluctant to hurt his feelings; for she knew instinctively he was very sensitive.

Her eyes and lips softened winningly.

Louis Joseph Vance

"It's so good of you to think of me," she said.

"You mean—you—you will come?" he cried, transported.

"I shall be very glad."

"That's—that's awf'ly kind of you," he said huskily. "Now, do please find some way to get rid of me."

Smiling quietly, the girl recovered the glove boxes.

"I'm afraid we haven't what you want in stock," she said in a voice not loud but clear enough to carry to the ears of her inquisitive co-labourers. "We're expecting a fresh shipment in next week—if you could stop in then...."

"Thank you very much," said P. Sybarite with uncalled-for emotion.

He backed away awkwardly, spoiled the effect altogether by lifting his hat, wheeled and broke for the doors....

IV

A LIKELY STORY

From the squalour, the heat, dirt and turmoil of Eighth
Avenue, P. Sybarite turned west on Thirty-eighth Street to
seek his boarding-house.

This establishment—between which and the Cave of the Smell
his existence alternated with the monotony of a pendulum—
was situated midway on the block on the north side of the
street. It boasted a front yard fenced off from the sidewalk with
a rusty railing: a plot of arid earth scantily tufted with grass,
suggesting that stage of baldness which finally precedes
complete nudity. Behind this, the moat-like area was spanned
to the front door by a ragged stoop of brownstone. The four-
story facade was of brick whose pristine coat of fair white paint
had aged to a dry and flaking crust, lending the house an
appearance distinctly eczematous.

The sun of April, declining, threw down the street a slant of
kindly light to mitigate its homeliness. In this ethereal
evanescence the house Romance took the air upon the stoop.

George Bross was eighty-five per-centum of the house
Romance. The remainder was Miss Violet Prim. Mr. Bross sat
a step or two below Miss Prim, his knees adjacent to his chin,
his face, upturned to his charmer, wreathed in a fond and
fatuous smile. From her higher plane, she smiled in like wise
down upon him. She seemed in the eyes of her lover unusually

fair—and was: Saturday was her day for seeming unusually fair; by the following Thursday there would begin to be a barely perceptible shadow round the roots of her golden hair....

She was a spirited and abundant creature, hopelessly healthy beneath the coat of paint, powder and peroxide with which she armoured herself against the battle of Life. Normally good-looking in ordinary daylight, she was a radiant beauty across footlights. Her eyes were bright even at such times as belladonna lacked in them; her nose pretty and pert; her mouth, open for laughter (as it usually was), disclosed twin rows of sound, white, home-made teeth. Her active young person was modelled on generous lines and, as a rule, clothed in a manner which, if inexpensive, detracted nothing from her conspicuous sightliness. She was fond of adorning her pretty, sturdy shoulders, as well as her fetching and shapely, if plump, ankles, with semi-transparent things—and she was quite as fond of having them admired.

P. Sybarite, approaching the gate, delicately averted his eyes....

At that moment, George was announcing in an undertone: "Here's the lollop now."

"You are certainly one observin' young gent," remarked Miss Prim in accents of envious admiration.

Ignoring the challenge, Bross pondered hastily. "Think I better spring it on him now?" he enquired in doubt.

"My Gawd, no!" protested the lady in alarm. "I'd spoil the plant, sure. I'd *love* to watch you feed it to him, but Heaven knows I'd never be able to hold in without bustin'."

"You think he'll swallow it, all right?"

"That simp?" cried Miss Prim in open derision. "Why, he'll eat it *alive!*"

P. Sybarite walked into the front yard, and the chorus lady began to crow with delight, welcoming him with wild wavings of a pretty, powdered forearm.

"Well, *look* who's here! 'Tis old George W. Postscript—as I live! Hitherwards, little one: I wouldst speech myself to thee."

Smiling, P. Sybarite approached the pair. He liked Miss Prim for her unaffected high spirits, and because he was never in the least ill at ease with her.

"Well?" he asked pleasantly, blinking up at the lady from the foot of the steps. "What is thy will, O Breaker of Hearts?"

"That'll be about all for yours," announced Violet reprovingly. "You hadn't oughta carry on like that—at your age, too! Not that *I* mind—I rather like it; but what'd your family say if they knew you was stuck on an actress?"

"Love blows as the wind blows," P. Sybarite quoted gently. "How shall I hide the fact of my infatuation? If my family cast me off, so be it!"

"I told you, behave! Next thing you know, George will be bitin' the fence.... What's all this about you givin' a box party at the Knickerbocker to-night?"

"It's a fact," affirmed P. Sybarite. "Only I had counted on the pleasure of inviting you myself," he added with a patient glance at George.

"Never mind about that," interposed the lady. "I'm just as tickled to death, and I love you a lot more'n I do George, anyway. So *that's* all right. Only I was afraid for a while he was connin' me."

"You feel better now?"

Violet placed a theatrical hand above her heart. "Such a relief!"

she declared intensely—"you'll never know!" Then she jumped up and wheeled about to the door with petticoats professionally a-swirl. "Well, if I'm goin' to do a stagger in society to-night, it's me to go doll myself up to the nines. So long!"

"Hold on!" George cried in alarm. "You ain't goin' to go dec—decol—low neck and all that? Cut it, kid: me and P.S. ain't got no dress soots, yunno."

"Don't fret," returned Violet from the doorway. "I know how to pretty myself for my comp'ny, all right. Besides, you'll be at the back of the box and nobody'll know you exist. Me and Molly Leasing'll get all the yearnin' stares."

She disappeared by way of the vestibule. George shook a head heavy with forebodings.

"Class to that kid, all right," he observed. "Some stepper, take it from me. Anyway, I'm glad it's a box: then I can hide under a chair. I ain't got nothin' to go in but these hand-me-downs."

"You'll be all right," said P. Sybarite hastily.

"Well, I won't feel lonely if you don't dress up like a horse. What are you going to wear, anyway?"

"A shave, a clean collar, and what I stand in. They're all I have."

"Then you got nothin' on me. What's your rush?"—as P. Sybarite would have passed on. "Wait a shake. I wanna talk to you. Sit down and have a cig."

There was a hint of serious intention in the manner of the shipping clerk to induce P. Sybarite, after the hesitation of an instant, to accede to his request. Squatting down upon the steps, he accepted a cigarette, lighted it, inhaled deeply.

"Well?"

"I dunno how to break it to you," Bross faltered dubiously. "You better brace yourself to lean up against the biggest disappointment ever."

P. Sybarite regarded him with sharp distrust. "You interest me strangely, George.... But perhaps you're no more addled than usual. Consider me gently prepared against the worst—and get it off your chest."

"Well," said George regretfully, "I just wanna put you next to the facts before you ask her. Miss Lessing ain't goin' to go with us to-night."

P. Sybarite looked startled and grieved.

"No?" he exclaimed.

George wagged his head mournfully. "It's a shame. I know you counted on it, but I guess you'll have to get summonelse."

"I'm afraid I don't understand. How do you know Miss Lessing won't go? Did she tell you so?"

"Not what you might call exactly, but she won't all right," George returned with confidence. "There ain't one chance in a hundred I'm in wrong."

"In wrong? How?"

"About her bein' who she is."

P. Sybarite subjected the open, naif countenance of the shipping clerk to a prolonged and doubting scrutiny.

"No, I ain't crazy in the head, neither," George asseverated with some heat. "I suspicioned somethin' was queer about that girl right along, but now I *know* it."

"Explain yourself."

"Ah, it ain't nothin' against her! You don't have to scorch your collar. *She's* all right. Only—she's in bad. I don't s'pose you seen the evenin' paper?"

"No."

"Well, I picked up the *Joinal* down to Clancey's—this is it." With an effective flourish, George drew the sheet from his coat pocket and unfolded its still damp and pungent pages. "And soon's I seen that," he added, indicating a smudged halftone, "I begun to wise up to that little girl. It's sure some shame about her, all right, all right."

Taking the paper, P. Sybarite examined with perplexity a portrait labelled "Marian Blessington." Whatever its original aspect, the coarse mesh of the reproducing process had blurred it to a vague presentment of the head and shoulders of almost any young woman with fair hair and regular features: only a certain, almost indefinable individuality in the pose of the head remotely suggested Molly Lessing.

In a further endeavour to fathom his meaning, the little bookkeeper conned carefully the legend attached to the putative likeness:

MARIAN BLESSINGTON

only daughter of the late Nathaniel Blessington, millionaire founder of the great Blessington chain of department stores. Although much sought after on account of the immense property into control of which she is to come on her twenty-fifth birthday, Miss Blessington contrived to escape matrimonial entanglement until last January, when Brian Shaynon, her guardian and executor of the Blessington estate, gave out the announcement of her engagement to his son, Bayard Shaynon. This engagement was whispered to be distasteful to the young woman, who is noted for her independent and spirited nature; and it is now persistently being rumoured that she had demonstrated her disapproval by disappearing mysteriously from the knowledge of her guardian. It is said that nothing has been known of her whereabouts since about the 1st of March, when she left her home in the Shaynon mansion on Fifth Avenue, ostensibly for a shopping tour. This was flatly contradicted this morning by Brian Shaynon, who in an interview with a reporter for the EVENING JOURNAL declared that his ward sailed for Europe February 28th on the *Mauretania*, and has since been in constant communication with her betrothed and his family. He also denied having employed detectives to locate his ward. The sailing list of the *Mauretania* fails to give the name of Miss Blessington on the date named by Mr. Shaynon.

Refolding the paper, P. Sybarite returned it without comment.

"Well?" George demanded anxiously.

"Well?"

"Ain't you hep yet?" George betrayed some little exasperation in addition to his disappointment.

"Hep?" P. Sybarite iterated wonderingly.

"Hep's the word," George affirmed: "John W. Hep, of the well-known family of that name—very closely related to the Jeremiah Wises. Yunno who I mean, don't you?"

"Sorry," said P. Sybarite sadly: "I'm not even distinctly connected with either family."

"You mean you don't make me?"

"God forestalled me there," protested P. Sybarite piously. "Inscrutable!"

Impatiently brushing aside this incoherent observation, George slapped the folded paper resoundingly in the palm of his hand.

"Then this here don't mean nothin' to you?"

"To me—nothing, as you say."

"You ain't dropped to the resemblance between Molly Lessing and Marian Blessington?"

"Between Miss Lessing and *that* portrait?" asked P. Sybarite scornfully.

"Why, they're dead ringers for each other. Any one what can't see that's blind."

"But I'm *not* blind."

"Well, then you gotta admit they look alike as twins—"

"But I've known twins who didn't look alike," said P.S.

"Ah, nix on the stallin'!" George insisted, on the verge of losing his emper. "Molly Lessing's the spit-'n'-image of Marian Blessington—and ou know it. What's more—look at their names? *Molly* for *Mary*—you ake that? *Mary* and *Marian's* near enough alike, ain't they? And hat's *Lessing* but *Blessington* docked goin' and comin'?"

"Wait a second. If I understand you, George, you're trying to imply that Miss Lessing is identical with Marian Blessington."

"You said somethin' then, all right."

"Simply because of the similarity of two syllables in their surnames and a fancied resemblance of Miss Lessing to this so-called portrait?"

"Now you're gettin' warm, P.S."

P.S. laughed quietly: "George, I've been doing you a grave injustice. I apologise."

George opened his eyes and emitted a resentful "*Huh?*"

"For years I've believed you were merely stupid," P.S. explained patiently. "Now you develop a famous, if fatuous, gift of imagination. I'm sorry. I apologise twice."

"Imag'nation hell!" Mr. Bross exploded. "Where's your own? It's plain's daylight what I say is so. When did Miss Lessing come here? Five weeks ago, to a day—March foist, or close onto it—just when the *Joinal* says she did her disappearin' stunt. How you goin' to get around that?"

"You forget that the *Journal* simply reports a rumour. It doesn't claim it's true. In fact, the story is contradicted by the very person that ought to know—Miss Blessington's guardian."

"Well, if she sailed for Europe on the *Mauretania*, like he says—how's it come her name wasn't on the passenger list?"

"It's quite possible that a young woman as much sought after and annoyed by fortune hunters, may have elected to sail incognita. It can be done, you know. In fact, it *has* been done."

George digested this in profound gloom.

"Then you don't believe what I'm tellin' you?"

"Not one-tenth of one iota of a belief."

George betrayed in a rude, choleric grunt, his disgust to see his splendid fabrication, so painfully concocted for the delusion and discomfiture of P. Sybarite, threatening to collapse of sheer intrinsic flimsiness. He had counted so confidently on the credulity of the little bookkeeper! And Violet had supported his confidence with so much assurance! Disgusting wasn't the word for George's emotions.

In desperation he grasped at one final, fugitive hope.

"All right," he said sullenly: "*all* right! You don't gotta believe me if you don't wanta. Only wait—that's all I ask—*wait*! You'll see I'm right when she turns down your invite to-night."

P. Sybarite smiled sunnily. "So that is why you thought she wouldn't go with us, is it?"

"You got me."

"You thought she, if Marian Blessington, must necessarily be such a snob that she wouldn't associate with poor devils like us, did you?"

"Wait. You'll see."

"Well, it's none of your business, George; but I don't mind telling you, you're wrong. Quite wrong. In the head, too, George. I've already asked Miss Lessing, and she has accepted."

George's eyes, protruding, glistened with poignant surprise.

"You ast her already?"

"That's why I left you down the street. I dropped into Blessington's for the sole purpose of asking her."

"And she fell for it?"

"She accepted my invitation—yes."

After a long pause George ground his cigarette beneath his heel, and rose.

"In wrong, as usual," he admitted with winning simplicity. "I never did guess *any*thin' right the first time. Only—you just grab this from me: maybe she's willin' to run the risk of bein' seen with us, but that ain't sayin' she's anybody but Marian Blessington."

"You really think it likely that Miss Blessington, hiding from her guardian and anxious to escape detection, would take a job at the glove counter of her own store, where everybody must know her by sight—where her guardian, Shaynon himself, couldn't fail to see her at least twice a day, as he enters and leaves the building?"

Staggered, Bross recovered quickly.

"That's just her cuteness. She doped it out the safest place for her would be the last place he'd look for her!"

"And you really think that she, accustomed to every luxury that money can buy, would voluntarily come down to living here, at six dollars a week, and clerking in a department store—simply because, according to the papers, she's opposed to a marriage that she can't be forced to contract in a free country like this?"

"Wel-l...." George floundered helplessly for a moment; and fell back again upon an imagination for the time being stimulated to an abnormal degree of inventiveness:

"P'raps old Shaynon's double-crossed her somehow we don't know nothin' about. He ain't above it, if all they tell of him's true. Maybe he's got her coin away from her, and she had to go to work for a livin'. Stranger things have happened in this burg, P.S."

It was the turn of P.S. to hesitate in doubt; or at all events, so George Bross inferred from a sudden change in the expression of the little man's eyes. Momentarily they seemed to cloud, as if in introspection. But he rallied quickly enough.

"All things are possible, George," he admitted with his quizzical grin. "But this time you're mistaken. I'm not arguing with you, George; I'm *telling* you: you're hopelessly mistaken."

"You think so—huh?" growled George. "Well, I got eight iron bucks that says Marian Blessington to any five of your money."

He made a bold show of his pay envelope.

"It'd be a shame to rob you, George," said P. Sybarite. "Besides, you're bad-tempered when broke."

"Never you mind about that. Here's my eight, if you've got five that makes a noise like Molly Lessing."

P. Sybarite laughed softly and produced the little wad of bills that represented his weekly wage. At this, George involuntarily drew back.

"And how would you settle the bet?"

"Leave it to her," insisted George in an expiring gasp of bravado.

"You'd ask her yourself?"

"Ye-es—"

"And let it stand on her answer?"

"Wel-l—"

"Here she comes now," added P. Sybarite, glancing up the street. "Quick, now; you've only a minute to decide. Is it a bet?"

With a gesture of brave decision, George returned his money to his pocket.

"You're an easy mark," he observed in accents of deep pity. "I knew you'd think I meant it."

"But didn't you, George?"

"Nah—nothin' like that! I was just kiddin' you along, to see how much you'd swallow."

"It's all right then," agreed P. Sybarite. "Only—George!"

"Huh?"

"Don't you breathe a word of this to Miss Lessing?"

"Why not?"

"Because I tell you not to—because," said P. Sybarite firmly, "I forbid you."

"You—you forbid me? Holy Mike! And what—"

"Sssh!" P. Sybarite warned him sibilantly. "Miss Lessing might hear you.... What will happen if you disobey me," he added as the shop girl turned in at the gateway, lowering his own voice and fixing the shipping clerk with a steely stare, "will be another accident, much resembling that of this afternoon—if you haven't forgotten. Now mind what I tell you, and be good."

Mr. Bross swelled with resentment; exhibited a distorted and empurpled visage; but kept silence.

V

THE COMIC SPIRIT

Pausing at the foot of the stoop, Miss Lessing looked up at the two young men and smiled.

"Good-evening," she said with a pretty nod for P. Sybarite; and, with its fellow for George, "Good-evening, Mr. Bross," she added.

Having acknowledged this salutation with that quaint courtesy which somehow seemed to fit him like a garment, P. Sybarite smiled strangely at the shipping clerk.

The latter mumbled something incoherent, glanced wildly toward the young woman, and spluttered explosively; all with a blush so deep that its effect was apoplectic.

Alarmed by this exhibition, Miss Lessing questioned P. Sybarite with her lifted brows and puzzled eyes.

"George is a little bit excited," he apologised. "Every so often he becomes obsessed with mad desire to impose upon some simple and credulous nature like mine. And failure always unbalances him. He becomes excitable—ah—irrational—"

With an inarticulate snort, Mr. Bross turned and fled into the house.

Confusion possessed him, and with it rage: stumbling blindly on the first flight of steps, he clawed the atmosphere with fingers that itched for vengeance.

"I'll get even!" he muttered savagely—"I'll get hunk with that boob if it's the last act of my life!"

Fortunately, the hall was gloomy and at that moment deserted.

On the first landing he checked, clutched the banisters for support, and endeavoured to compose himself—but with less success than he realised.

It was with a suggestion of stealth that he ascended the second flight—with an enforced deliberateness and caution that were wasted. For as he reached the top, the door of the back hall-bedroom opened gently for the space of three inches. Through this aperture were visible a pair of bright eyes, with the curve of a plump and pretty cheek, and an adorable bare arm and shoulder.

"That you, George?" Violet Prim demanded with vivacity.

Reluctantly he stopped and in a throaty monosyllable admitted his identity.

"Well, how'd it go off?"

"Fine!"

"He fell for it?"

"All over himself. Honest, Vi, it was a scream to watch his eyes pop. You could've clubbed 'em outa his bean without touchin' his beak. I 'most died."

Miss Prim giggled appreciatively.

"You're a wonder, George," she applauded. "It takes you to

think 'em out."

"Ah, I don't know," returned her admirer with becoming modesty.

"He's gone on her, all right, ain't he?"

"Crazy about her!"

"Think he'll make a play for her now?"

George demurred. Downright lying was all very well; he could manage that with passable craft, especially when, as in this instance, detection would be difficult; but prophecy was a little out of his line. Though with misgivings, he resorted to unvarnished truth:

"You never can tell about P.S. He's a queer little gink."

Footsteps became audible on the stairs below.

"Well, so long. See you at dinner," George added in haste.

"George!"

"Well?" he asked, delaying with ill grace.

"What makes you sound so funny?"

"Laughin'!" protested George convincingly.

With determination and a heavy tread he went on to his room.

VI

SPRING TWILIGHT

When he had shaved (with particular care) and changed his linen (trimming collar and cuffs to a degree of uncommon nicety) and resumed his coat (brushing and hating it simultaneously and with equal ferocity, for its very shabbiness) P. Sybarite sought out a pipe old and disreputable enough to be a comfort to any man, and sat down by the one window of his room (top floor, hall, back) to smoke and consider the state of the universe while awaiting the dinner gong.

The window commanded an elevated if non-exhilarating view of back yards, one and all dank, dismal, and littered with the debris of a long, hard winter. Familiarity, however, had rendered P. Sybarite immune to the miasma of melancholy they exhaled; the trouble in his patient blue eyes, the wrinkles that lined his forehead, owned another cause.

In fact, George had wrought more disastrously upon his temper than P. Sybarite had let him see. His hints, innuendoes, and downright assertions had in reality distilled a subtle poison into the little man's humour. For in spite of his embattled incredulity and the clear reasoning with which he had overborne George's futile insistence, there still lingered in his mind (and always would, until he knew the truth himself) a carking doubt.

Perhaps it was true. Perhaps George had guessed shrewdly.

Perhaps Molly Lessing of the glove counter really was one and the same with Marian Blessington of the fabulous fortune.

Old Brian Shaynon was a known devil of infinite astuteness; it would be quite consistent with his character and past performances if, despairing of gaining control of his ward's money by urging her into unwelcome matrimony with his son, he had contrived to over-reach her in some manner, and so driven her to become self-supporting.

Perhaps hardly likely: the hypothesis was none the less quite plausible; a thing had happened, within P. Sybarite's knowledge of Brian Shaynon....

Even if George's romance were true only in part, these were wretched circumstances for a girl of gentle birth and rearing to adopt. It was really a shocking boarding-house. P. Sybarite had known it intimately for ten years; use had made him callous to its shortcomings; but he was not yet so far gone that he could forget how unwholesome and depressing it must seem to one accustomed to better things. He could remember most vividly how he had loathed it for weeks, months, and years after the tide of evil fortunes had cast him upon its crumbling brownstone stoop (even in that distant day, crumbling).

Now, however ... P. Sybarite realised suddenly that habit had instilled into his bosom a sort of mean affection for the grim and sordid place. Time had made him sib to its spirit, close to its niggard heart. Scarcely a nook or corner of it with which he was not on terms of the most intimate acquaintance. In the adjoining room a deserted woman had died by her own hand; her moans, filtered through the dividing wall, had summoned P. Sybarite—too late. The double front room on the same floor harboured an amiable couple whose sempiternal dissensions only his tact and persistence ever served to still. The other hall-bedroom had housed for many years a dipsomaniac whose periodic orgies had cost P. Sybarite many a night of bedside vigil. On the floor below lived a maiden lady whose quenchless hopes still centred about his amiable person.

Downstairs in the clammy parlour he had whiled away unnumbered hours assisting at dreary "bridge drives," or playing audience to amateur recitals on the aged and decrepit "family organ." For an entire decade he had occupied the same chair at the same table in the basement dining-room, feasting on beef, mutton, Irish stew, ham-and-beans, veal, pork, or just-hash—according to the designated day of the week....

The very room in which he sat was somehow dear to him; upon it he wasted a sentiment in a way akin to that with which one regards the grave of a beloved friend; it was, in fact, the tomb of his own youth. Its narrow and impoverished bed had groaned with the restless weight of him all those many nights through which he had lain wakeful, in impotent mutiny against the outrageous circumstances that made him a prisoner there. Its walls had muted the sighs in which the desires of youth had been spent. Its floor matting was worn threadbare with the impatient pacings of his feet (four strides from door to window: swing and repeat *ad libitum*). Its solitary gas-jet had, with begrudged illumination, sicklied o'er the pages of those innumerable borrowed books with which he had sought to dull poignant self-consciousness....

A tomb!... Bitterly he granted the aptness of that description of his cubicle: mausoleum of his every hope and aspiration, sepulchre of all his ability and promise. In this narrow room his very self had been extinguished: a man had degenerated into a machine. Everything that caught his eye bore mute witness to this truth: the shabby tin alarm clock on the battered bureau was one of a dynasty that had roused him at six in the morning with unfailing regularity three hundred and sixty-five times per year (Sundays were too rare in his calendar and too precious to be wasted abed). From an iron hook in the window frame dangled the elastic home-exerciser with which it was his unfailing habit to perform a certain number of matutinal contortions, to keep his body wholesome and efficient. Beneath the bed was visible the rim of a shallow English tub that made possible his subsequent sponge bath....

A machine; a fixture; creature of an implacable routine; a spirit immolated upon the altar of habit: into this he had degenerated in ten years. Such was the effect of life in this melancholy shelter for the homeless wage-slave. He was no lonely victim. In his term he had seen many another come in hope, linger in disappointment, leave only to go to a meaner cell in the same stratum of misfortune.

Was this radiant spirit of youth and gentle loveliness (who might, for all one knew to the contrary, be Marian Blessington after all) to be suffered to become one of that disconsolate crew?

What could be done to prevent it?

Nothing that the wits of P. Sybarite could compass: he was as inefficient as any gnat in any web....

Through the halls resounded the cacophonous clangour of a cracked gong announcing dinner. Sighing, P. Sybarite rose and knocked the ashes delicately from his pipe—saving the dottle for a good-night whiff after the theatre.

Being Saturday, it was the night of ham-and-beans. P. Sybarite loathed ham-and-beans with a deathly loathing. Nevertheless he ate his dole of ham-and-beans. He sat on the landlady's right, and was reluctant to hurt her feelings or incur her displeasure. Besides, he was hungry: between the home-exerciser and the daily walks to and from the Brooklyn Bridge, his normal appetite was that of an athlete in pink of training.

Miss Lessing sat on the same side of the main dining-table, but half a dozen chairs away. P. Sybarite couldn't see her save by craning his neck. He refused to crane his neck: it might seem ostentatious.

Violet and her George occupied adjoining chairs at another and smaller table. Their attendance was occasionally manifested through the medium of giggles and guffaws. P. Sybarite envied them: he had it in his heart to envy anybody young enough to be able to see a joke at that dinner table.

By custom, the landlady relinquished her seat some minutes in advance of any guest. When P. Sybarite left the room he found her established at a desk in the basement hallway. Pausing, he delivered unto her the major portion of his week's wage. Setting aside another certain amount against the cost of laundry work, tobacco, and incidentals, he had five dollars left....

He wondered if he dared risk the extravagance of a modest supper after the theatre; and knew he dared not—knew it in wretchedness of spirit, cursing his fate....

There remained half an hour to be killed before time to start for the theatre. George Bross joined him on the stoop. They smoked pensively, while the afterglow faded from the western sky and veil after veil of shadow crept stealthily out of the east, masking the rectangular, utilitarian ugliness of the street, deepening its dusk to darkness. Street lamps, touched by the flame-tipped wand of a belated lamplighter, bourgeoned spasmodically like garish flowers of the metropolitan night. Across the way gas-lit windows glowed like squares on some great, blurred checker-board. The roadway teemed with shrieking children. Somewhere—near at hand—a pianola lost its temper and whaled the everlasting daylights out of an inoffensive melody from "The Pink Lady." Other, more diffident instruments tinkled apologetically in the distance. Intermittently, across the gaunt scaffolding of the Ninth Avenue L, at one end of the block, roaring trains flashed long chains of lights. On the other hand, Eighth Avenue buzzed resonantly in stifling clouds of incandescent dust. The air smelt of warm asphalt....

And it was Spring: the tenth Spring P. Sybarite had watched from that self-same spot.

Discontent bred in him a brooding despondency. He felt quite sure that the realists were right about Life: it wasn't worth living, after all.

The prospect of the theatre lost its attraction. He was sure he wouldn't enjoy it. Such silly romantical nonsense was out of tune with the immortal Truth about Things, which he had just discovered: Life was a poor Joke....

At his side, George Bross, on his behalf, was nursing his private and personal grouch. Between them they manufactured an atmosphere of gloom that would have done credit to a brace of dumb Socialists.

But presently Miss Prim and Miss Lessing appeared, and changed all that in a twinkling.

VII

AFTERMATH

"Well," observed Violet generously, "I thought little me was pretty well stage-broke; but I gotta hand it to Otis. He's *some* actor. He had me going from the first snore."

"Some actor is *right*," affirmed Mr. Bross with conviction, "and some show, too, if you wanta know. I could sit through it twicet. Say, I couldn't quit thinkin' what a grand young time I'd start in this old burg if I could only con this *Kismet* thing into slippin' me *my* Day of Days. Believe me or not, there would be *a* party."

"What would you do?" asked Molly Lessing, smiling.

"Well, the first flop I'd nail down all the coin that was handy, and then I'd buy me a flock of automobiles—and have a table reserved for me at the Knickerbocker for dinner every night— and...." Imagination flagged. "Well," he concluded defensively, "I can tell you one thing I wouldn't do."

"What?" demanded Violet.

"I wouldn't let any ward politician like that there *Wazir*, or whatever them A-rabs called him, kid me into trying to throw a bomb at Charlie Murphy—or anythin' like that. No-oh! Not this infant. That's where your friend *Hajj the Beggar's* foot slipped on him. Up to then he had everythin' his own way. If

Louis Joseph Vance

he'd only had sense enough to stall, he'd've wound up in a blaze of glory."

"But, you bonehead," Violet argued candidly, "he had to. That was his part: it was written in the play."

"G'wan. If he'd just stalled round and refused to jump through, the author'd 've framed up some other way out. Why—blame it!—he'd've *had* to!"

"That will be about all for me," said Violet. "I don't feel strong enough to-night to stand any more of your dramatic criticism. Lead me home—and please talk baseball all the way."

With a resentful grunt, Mr. Bross clamped a warm, moist hand round the plump arm of his charmer, and with masterful address propelled her from the curb in front of the theatre, where the little party had paused, to the northwest corner of Broadway: their progress consisting in a series of frantic rushes broken by abrupt pauses to escape annihilation in the roaring after-theatre crush of motor-cars. P. Sybarite, moving instinctively to follow, leaped back to the sidewalk barely in time to save his toes a crushing beneath the tires of a hurtling taxicab.

He smiled a furtive apology at Molly Lessing, who had demonstrated greater discretion, and she returned his smile in the friendliest manner. His head was buzzing—and her eyes were kind. Neither spoke; but for an instant he experienced a breathless sense of sympathetic isolation with her, there on that crowded corner, elbowed and shouldered in the eddy caused by the junction of the outpouring audience with the midnight tides of wayfarers surging north and south.

The wonder and the romance of the play were still warm and vital, in his imagination, infusing his thoughts with a roseate glamour of unreality, wherein all things were strangely possible. The iridescent imagery of the Arabian Nights of his boyhood (who has forgotten the fascination of those three fat old volumes of crabbed type, illuminated with their hundreds of cramped old wood-cuts?) had in a scant three hours been recreated for him by Knoblauch's fantastic drama with its splendid investment of scene and costume, its admirable histrionic interpretation, and the robust yet exquisitely tempered artistry of Otis Skinner. For three hours he had forgotten his lowly world, had lived on the high peaks of romance, breathing only their rare atmosphere that never was on land or sea.

Difficult he found it now, to divest his thoughts of that enthrallment, to descend to cold and sober reality, to remember he was a clerk, his companion a shop-girl, rather than a Prince disguised as Calander esquiring a Princess dedicated to Fatal Enchantment—that Kismet was a quaint fallacy, one with that whimsical conceit of Orient fatalism which assigns to each and every man his Day of Days, wherein he shall range the skies and plumb the abyss of his Destiny, alternately its lord and its puppet.

But presently, with an effort, blinking, he pulled his wits together; and a traffic policeman creating a favourable opening, the two scurried across and plunged into the comparative obscurity of West Thirty-eighth Street: sturdy George and his modest Violet already a full block in advance.

Discovering this circumstance by the glimmer through the shadows of Violet's conspicuously striped black-and-white taffeta, P. Sybarite commented charitably upon their haste.

"If we hurry we might catch up," suggested Molly Lessing.

"I don't miss 'em much," he admitted, without offering to mend the pace.

She laughed softly.

"Are they really in love?"

"George is," replied P. Sybarite, after taking thought.

"You mean she isn't?"

"To blush unseen is Violet's idea of nothing to do—not, at least, when one is a perfect thirty-eight and possesses a good digestion and an infinite capacity for amusement *a la carte*."

"That is to say—?" the girl prompted.

"Violet will marry well, if at all."

"Not Mr. Bross, then?"

"Nor any other poor man. I don't say she doesn't care for George, but before anything serious comes of it he'll have to make good use of his Day of Days—if *Kismet* ever sends him one. I hope it will," P. Sybarite added sincerely.

"You don't believe—really—?"

"Just now? With all my heart! I'm so full of romantic nonsense I can hardly stick. Nothing is too incredible for me to believe to-night. I'm ready to play *Hajj the Beggar* to any combination of impossibilities *Kismet* cares to brew in Bagdad-on-the-Hudson!"

Again the girl laughed quietly to his humour.

"And since you're a true believer, Mr. Sybarite, tell me, what use *you* would make of your Day of Days?"

"I? Oh, I—" Smiling wistfully, he opened deprecatory palms. "Hard to say.... I'm afraid I should prove a fatuous fool in George's esteem equally with old *Hajj*. I'm sure that, like him, the sunset of my Day would see me proscribed, a price upon my head."

"But—why?"

"I'm afraid I'd try to use my power to right old wrongs."

After a pause, she asked diffidently: "Your own?"

"Perhaps.... Yes, my own, certainly.... And perhaps another's, not so old but possibly quite as grievous."

"Somebody you care for a great deal?"

Thus tardily made to realise into what perils his fancy was leading him, he checked and weighed her question with his answer, gravely judgmatical.

"Perhaps I'd better not say that," he announced, a grin tempering his temerity; "but I'd go far for a friend, somebody who had been kind to me, and—ah—tolerant—if she were in trouble and could use my services."

He fancied her glance was quick and sharp and searching; but her voice when she spoke was even and lightly attuned to his whimsical mood.

"Then you're not even sure she—your friend—is in trouble?"

"I've an intuition: she wouldn't be where she is if she wasn't."

Her laughter at this absurdity was delightful; whether with him or at him, it was infectious; he echoed it without misgivings.

"But—seriously—you're not sure, are you, Mr. Sybarite?"

"Only, Miss Lessing," he said soberly, "of my futile, my painfully futile good will."

She seemed to start to speak, to think better of it, to fall silent in sudden, shy constraint. He stole a side-long glance, troubled, wondering if perhaps he had ventured too impudently, pursuing his whim to the point of trespass upon the inviolable confines of her reserve.

She wore a sweet, grave face, *en profile*; her eyes veiled with long lashes, the haunts of tender shadows; her mouth of gracious lips unsmiling, a little triste. Compunctions smote him; with his crude and clumsy banter he had contrived to tune her thoughts to sadness. He would have given worlds to undo that blunder; to show her that he had meant neither a rudeness nor a wish to desecrate her reticence, but only an indirect assurance of gratitude to her for suffering him and willingness to serve her within the compass of his poverty-stricken powers. For in retrospect his invitation assumed the proportions of an importunity, an egregious piece of presumption: so that he could have groaned to contemplate it.

He didn't groan, save inwardly; but respected her silence, and held his own in humility and mortification of spirit until they were near the dooryard of their boarding-house. And even then it was the girl who loosed his tongue.

"Why—where are they?" she asked in surprise.

Startled out of the deeps of self-contempt, P. Sybarite discovered that she meant Violet and George, who were nowhere visible.

"Violet said something about a little supper in her room," explained the girl.

"I know," he replied: "crackers and cheese, beer and badinage: our humble pleasures. You'll be bored to extinction—but you'll come, won't you?"

"Why, of course! I counted on it. But—"

"They must have hurried on to make things ready—Violet to set her room to rights, George to tote the wash-pitcher to the corner for the beer. And very likely, pending our arrival, they're lingering at the head of the stairs for a kiss or two."

The girl paused at the gate. "Then we needn't hurry," she suggested, smiling.

"We needn't delay," he countered amiably. "If somebody doesn't interrupt 'em before long, George will be too late to get the pitcher filled. This town shuts up tight at midnight, Saturdays—if you want to believe everything you hear. So there's no need of being too indulgent with our infatuated fellow-inmates."

"But—just a minute, Mr. Sybarite," she insisted.

"As many as you wish," he laughed. "As a matter of fact, I loathe draught beer."

"Do be serious," she begged. "I want to thank you."

He was aware of a proffered hand, slender and fine in a shabby glove; and took it in his own, uneasily conscious of a curious disturbance in his bosom, of a strange and not unpleasant sense of commingled expectancy, pleasure, and diffidence (as far as he was able to analyse it—or cared to—at that instant).

"It was kind of you to come," he said jerkily, in his embarrassment.

"I enjoyed every moment," she said warmly. "But that wasn't all I meant when I thanked you."

His eyebrows climbed with surprise.

"What else, Miss Lessing?"

"Your delicacy in letting me know you understood—"

Disengaging her hand, she broke off with a startled movement, and a low cry of surprise.

A taxicab, swinging into the street from Eighth Avenue, had

Louis Joseph Vance

boiled up to the curb before the gate, and pausing, discharged a young man in a hurry; witness the facts that he had the door open when halfway between the corner and the house, and was on the running-board before the vehicle was fairly at a halt.

In a stride this one crossed the sidewalk and pulled up, silently, trying to master the temper which was visibly shaking him. Tall, well-proportioned, impressively turned out in evening clothes, he thrust forward a handsome face marred by an evil, twisted mouth, and peered searchingly at the girl.

Instinctively she shrank back inside the fence, eyeing him with a look of fascinated dismay.

As instinctively P. Sybarite bristled between the two.

"Well?" he snapped at the intruder.

An impatient gesture of a hand immaculately gloved in white abolished him completely—as far, at least, as the other was concerned.

"Ah—Miss Lessing, I believe?"

The voice was strong and musical but poisoned with a malicious triumph that grated upon the nerves of P. Sybarite; he declined to be abolished.

"Say the word," he suggested serenely to the girl, "and I'll bundle this animal back into that taxi and direct the driver to the nearest accident ward. I'd rather like to, really."

"Get rid of this microbe," interrupted the other savagely— "unless you want him buried between glass slides under a microscope."

The girl turned to P. Sybarite with pleading eyes and imploring hands.

"If you please, dear Mr. Sybarite," she begged in a tremulous voice: "I'm afraid I must speak alone with this"—there was a barely perceptible pause—gentleman. If you won't mind waiting a moment—at the door—?"

"If it pleases you, Miss Lessing—most certainly." He drew back a step or two. "But speaking of microbes," he added incisively, "a word of advice: don't tease 'em. My bite is deadly: neither Pasteur nor your family veterinary could save you."

Ignored by the man, but satisfied in his employment of the last word, he strutted back to the brownstone stoop, there to establish himself, out of earshot but within, easy hail.

Hearing nothing, he made little more of the guarded conference that began on his withdrawal. The man, entering the dooryard, had cornered the girl in an angle of the fence. He seemed at once insistent, determined, and thoroughly angry; while she exhibited perfect composure with some evident contempt and implacable obstinacy. Nevertheless, in a brace of minutes the fellow seemingly brought forth some telling argument. She wavered and her accents rose in doubt:

"Is that true?"

His reply, if inaudible, was as forcible as it was patently an affirmative.

"I don't believe you!"

"You don't dare doubt me."

This time he was clearly articulate, and betrayed a conviction that he had won the day: an impression borne out by the evident irresolution of the girl, prefacing her abrupt surrender.

"Very well," she said in a tone of resignation.

"You'll go?"

"Yes."

He moved aside, to give her way through the gate. But she hung back, with a glance for P. Sybarite.

"One moment, please," she said: "I must leave a message."

"Nonsense—!"

She showed displeasure in the lift of her chin. "I think I'm my own mistress—as yet."

He growled indistinguishably.

"You have my promise," she cut him short coldly. "Wait for me." And she turned back to the house.

Wondering, P. Sybarite went to meet her. Impulsively she gave him her hand a second time; with as little reflection, he took it in both his own.

"Is there nothing I can do?"

Her voice was broken: "I don't know. I must go—it's imperative.... Could you—?... I wonder!"

"Anything you ask," he asserted confidently.

Hesitating briefly, in a tone little above a whisper: "I must go," she repeated. "I can't refuse. But—alone. Do you understand—?"

"You mean—without him?" P. Sybarite nodded toward the man fuming in the gateway.

"Yes. If you could suggest something to detain him long enough for me to get into the cab and say one word to the chauffeur—"

The chest of P. Sybarite swelled.

"Leave it to me," he said with fine simplicity.

"Molly!" cried the man at the gate.

"Don't answer," P. Sybarite advised: "if you don't, he'll lose patience and come to fetch you. And then—"

"But I'm afraid he may—"

"*Molly!*"

"Don't you fear for me: God's good to the Irish."

"MOLLY!"

"Do be quiet," suggested P. Sybarite, not altogether civilly.

The other started as if slapped.

"What's that?" he barked in a rage.

"I said, hold your tongue."

"The devil you did!" With a snort the man strode in to the stoop. "Do you know who you're talking to?" he demanded wrathfully, towering over P. Sybarite, momentarily forgetful of the girl.

Stepping aside, as if in alarm, she moved behind the fellow, and darted through the gate.

"I don't," P. Sybarite admitted amiably; "but your nose annoys me."

He fixed that feature with an irritating glare.

"You impudent puppy!" stormed the other. "Who are you?"

"Who—me?" echoed P. Sybarite in surprise. (The girl was now instructing the chauffeur.) "Why," he drawled, "I'm the guy that put the point in disappointment. Sure you've heard of *me?*"

At the curb, the door of the taxicab closed with a slam. Simultaneously the drone of the motor thickened to a rumble. The man with the twisted mouth turned just in time to see it drawing away.

"*Hi!*" he cried in surprise and dismay.

But the taxi didn't pause; to the contrary, it stretched out toward Ninth Avenue at a quickening pace.

With profanity appreciating the fact that he had been tricked, he picked up his heels in pursuit. But P. Sybarite had not finished with him. Deftly plucking the man back by the tail of his full-skirted opera coat, he succeeded in arresting his flight before it was fairly started.

"Here!" he protested. "What's your hurry?"

With a vicious snarl, the man turned and snatched at his cloak. But P. Sybarite adhered tenaciously to the coat.

"We were discussing your nose—"

At discretion, he interrupted himself to duck beneath the swing of a powerful fist. And this last, failing to find a mark, threw its owner off his balance. Tripping awkwardly over the low curbing of the dooryard walk, he reeled and went a-sprawl on his knees, while his hat fell off and (such is the impish habit of toppers) rolled and bounded several feet away.

Releasing the cloak, P. Sybarite withdrew to a respectful remove and held himself coolly alert against reprisals that never came. The other picked himself up quickly, cast about for the taxicab, discovered it swiftly making off—already twenty yards distant—and with a howl of rage bounded through the gate and gave chase at the top of his speed.

Gravely, P. Sybarite retrieved the hat and followed to the curbing.

"Hey!" he shouted after the fast retreating figure—"here's your *hat*!"

But he wasted breath. The taxicab was nearing Ninth Avenue, its pursuer sprinting bravely a hundred feet to the rear, and as he watched, both turned the northern corner and vanished like shapes of dream.

Sighing, P. Sybarite went back to the stoop and sat down to consider the state of his soul (which was vain-glorious) and the condition of the hat (which was soiled, rumpled, and disreputable).

VIII

WHEELS OF CHANCE

Turning the affair over in his mind, and considering it from every imaginable angle, P. Sybarite decided (fairly enough) that it was, on the whole, mysterious; lending at least some colour of likelihood to George's gratuitous guess-work.

Certainly it would seem that one had now every right to assume Miss Molly Lessing to be other than as she chose to seem; nowadays the villain in shining evening dress doesn't pursue the shrinking shop-girl save through the action of the obsolescent mellerdrammer or of the ubiquitous moving-picture reel. So much must at least be said for these great educators: they have broken the villain of his open-face attire; to-day he knows better, and when prowling to devour, disguises himself in the guileless if nobby "sack suit" of the widely advertised Kollege Kut brand....

In short, Molly Lessing might very well be Marian Blessington, after all!

In which case the man with the twisted mouth was, more probably than not, none other than that same Bayard Shaynon whom the young lady was reported to have jilted so arbitrarily.

Turning the topper over in his hands, it occurred to P. Sybarite to wonder if he did not, in it, hold a valuable clue to this riddle of identity. Promptly he took the hat indoors to find out, investigating it most thoroughly by the flickering, bluish glare of the lonely gas-jet that burned in the hallway.

It was a handsome and heavy hat of English manufacture, as witness the name of a Bond Street hatter in its crown; by the slight discolouration of its leather, had seen service without, however, depreciating in utility, needing only brushing and ironing to restore its pristine brilliance; carried neither name nor initials on its lining; and lacked every least hint as to its ownership—or so it seemed until the prying fingers of P. Sybarite turned down the leather and permitted a visiting card concealed therein to flutter to the floor.

The hall rack was convenient; hanging up the hat, P. Sybarite picked up the card. It displayed in conventional script the name, *Bailey Penfield*, with the address, *97 West 45th Street*; one corner, moreover, bore a pencilled hieroglyphic which seemed to read: "*O.K.—B.P.*"

"Whatever," P. Sybarite mused, "*that* may mean."

He turned the card over and examined its unmarked and taciturn reverse.

Stealthy footsteps on the stairs distracted his studious attention from the card. He looked up, blinking and frowning thoughtfully, to see George descending with the wash-pitcher wrapped in, but by no means disguised by, brown paper. Once at the bottom of the stairs, this one expressed amazement in a whisper, to avoid rousing their landlady, who held, unreasonably, that it detracted from the tone of her establishment for gentlemen boarders to rush the growler....

"Hel-lo! We thought you must've got lost in the shuffle."

"Did you?" said P. Sybarite absently.

"Where's Molly?"

"Miss Lessing?" P. Sybarite looked surprised. "Isn't she upstairs—with Violet?"

"No!"

"That's funny...."

"Why, when'd she leave you?"

"Oh, ten minutes ago, or so."

"She must have stopped in her room for somethin'."

"Perhaps."

"But why didn't you come on up?"

"Well, you see, I met a man outside I wanted to talk to for a moment. So I left her at the door."

"Well, Vi's waitin'. Run on up. I won't be five minutes. And knock on Molly's door and see what's the matter."

"All right," returned P. Sybarite serenely.

His constructive mendacity light upon his conscience, he permitted George time enough to leave the house and gain Clancey's, then quietly followed as far as the gate, from which point he cut across the southern sidewalk, turned west to Ninth Avenue, and there north to Forty-second Street, where he boarded a cross-town car.

This was quite the most insane freak in which he had indulged himself these many years; and frankly admitting this much, he was rather pleased than otherwise. He was bound to call on Mr. Bailey Penfield and inform that gentleman where he might find his hat. Incidentally he hoped to surprise something or other informing with regard to the fortunes of Miss Lessing subsequent to her impulsive flight by taxicab.

All of which, he calmly admitted, constituted an inexcusable impertinence: he deserved a thoroughgoing snubbing, and rather anticipated one, especially if destined to find Mr. Penfield at home or, by some vagary of chance, to encounter Miss Lessing again.

But he smiled cheerfully in contemplation of this prospect, buoyed up with a belief that his unconsciously idiotic behaviour was intrinsically more or less Quixotic, and further excited by the hope that he might possibly be permitted to serve his lady of mystery.

At all events, he meant to know more about Mr. Bailey Penfield before he slept.

Alighting at Sixth Avenue, he walked to Forty-fifth Street, turned off to the right, and in another moment was at a standstill, in the extremest perplexity, before Number 97.

By every normal indication, the house was closed and tenantless. From roof to basement its every window was blind with shades close-drawn. The front doors were closed, the basement grating likewise. An atmospheric accumulation of street debris littered the area flagstones, together with one or two empty and battered ash-cans, in whose shadows an emaciated cat skulked apprehensively. The one thing lacking to signify that the Penfield menage had moved bodily to the country, was the shield of a burglar protective association in one of the parlour windows. P. Sybarite looked for that in vain.

Disappointed in the conviction that he had drawn a false lead, the little man strolled on eastward a little distance, then on sheer impulse, gave up his project and, swinging about, started to go home. But now, as he approached Number 97 the second time, a taxicab turned in from Sixth Avenue, slid to the curb before that dwelling, and set down a smallish young man dressed in the extreme of fashion—a person of physical characteristics by no means to be confused with those of the man with the twisted mouth—who, negligently handing a bill to the chauffeur, ran nimbly up the steps, rang the door-bell, and promptly letting himself into the vestibule, closed the door behind him.

The taxicab swung round and made off. Not so P. Sybarite. Profoundly intrigued, he waited hopefully for this second midnight caller to reappear, as baffled as himself. But though he dawdled away a patient five minutes, nothing of the sort occurred. The front doors remained closed and undisturbed, as little communicative as the darkened windows.

Here was mystery within mystery, indeed! The circumstances annoyed P. Sybarite intensely. And why (he asked himself, with impatience) need he remain outside when another entered without let or hindrance?

Upon this thought he turned boldly up the steps, pressed the bell-button; laid hold of the door-knob, and entered into a vestibule as dark as his bewilderment and as empty as the palm of his hand; proving that the young gentleman of fashion had experienced no difficulty in penetrating farther into fastnesses of this singular establishment. And reflecting that where one had gone, another might follow, P. Sybarite pulled the door to behind him.

Instantly the bare and narrow vestibule was flooded with the merciless glare of half a dozen electric bulbs; and at the same time he found himself sustaining the intent scrutiny of a pair of inhospitable dark eyes set in an impassive dark face—this last abruptly disclosed in the frame of a small grille in one of the inner doors.

Though far too dumfounded for speech, he contrived to return the stare with aggressive interest, and to such effect that he presently wore through the patience of the other.

"Well?" he was gruffly asked.

"The Saints be praised!" returned P. Sybarite. "I find myself so. And yourself?" he added civilly: not to be outdone, as the saying is.

"What do you want?"

Irritating discourtesy inhered in the speaker's tone. P. Sybarite stiffened his neck.

"To see Mr. Penfield," he returned firmly—"of course!"

"What Mr. Penfield?" asked the other, after a pause so transient that it was little more than distinguishable, but which to P. Sybarite indicated beyond question that at least one Mr. Penfield was known to his cautious interlocutor.

"Mr. Bailey Penfield," he replied. "Who else?"

During a pause slightly longer than the first, the hostile and suspicious eyes summed him up a second time.

"No such party here," was the verdict. The man drew back and made as if to shut the grille.

"Nonsense!" P. Sybarite insisted sharply. "I have his card with this number—got it from him only to-night."

"Card?" The face returned to the grille.

P. Sybarite made no bones about displaying his alleged credential.

"I believe you'll find that authentic," he observed with asperity.

By way of answer, the grille closed with a snap; but his inclination to kick the door was nullified when, without further delay, it opened to admit him. Nose in air, he strutted in, and the door clanged behind him.

"Gimme another slant at that card," the guardian insisted.

Surrendering it with elaborate indifference, P. Sybarite treated himself to a comprehensive survey of the place.

He stood in the main hall of an old-fashioned residence. To his right, a double doorway revealed a drawing-room luxuriously furnished but, as far as he could determine, quite untenanted. On the left, a long staircase hugged the wall, with a glow of warm light at its head. To the rear, the hall ended in a single doorway through which he could see a handsome mahogany buffet elaborately arranged with shimmering damask, silver, and crystal.

"It's all right," announced the warden of the grille, his suspicions to all seeming completely allayed. "Mr. Penfield ain't in just at present, but"—here he grinned shrewdly—"I reckon you ain't so dead set on seein' him as you made out."

"On the contrary," P. Sybarite retorted stiffly, "my business is immediate and personal with Mr. Penfield. I will wait."

"Sure." Into the accents of the other there crept magically a trace of geniality. "Will you go right on up, or would you like a bite of somethin' to eat first?"

At the mere hint of food, a frightful pang of hunger transfixed P. Sybarite. He winked furtively, afraid to trust Iris tongue to speech.

"What d'ya say?" insinuated the doorkeeper. "Just a bit of a snack, eh? Say a caviare sandwich and a thimbleful of the grape?"

Abandoning false pride, P. Sybarite yielded:

"I don't mind if I do, thank you."

"Straight on back; Pete'll take care of you, all right."

A thumb indicated the door in the rear of the hall. Thither P. Sybarite betook himself on the instant, spurred by the demands of an appetite insatiable once it had won recognition.

He found the back room one of good proportions: whatever the architect's original intention, now serving as a combined lounge and grill, richly and comfortably furnished in sober, masculine fashion, boasting in all three buffets set forth with a lavish display of food and drink. In one of many deeply upholstered club chairs a gentleman of mature years and heavy body, with a scarlet face and a crumpled, wine-stained shirt-bosom, was slumbering serenely, two-thirds of an extravagant cigar cold between his fingers. In others two young men were confabulating quietly but with a most dissipated air, heads together over a brace of glasses. At a corner service table a negro in a white jacket was busy with a silver chafing-dish which exhaled a tantalising aroma. This last, at the entrance of P. Sybarite, glanced quickly over his shoulder, and seeing a strange face, clapped the cover on the steaming chafing-dish and discovered a round black countenance bisected by a complete mouthful of the most brilliant teeth imaginable.

"Yas-suh—comin'!" he gabbled cheerfully. "It's sho' a pleasure to see yo' again."

"At least," suggested P. Sybarite, dropping into a chair, "it will be, next time."

"Tha's right, suh—that's the troof!" The negro placed a small table adjacent to his elbow. "Tha's what Ah allus says to strange gemmun, fust time they comes hyeh, suh; makes 'em feel more at home like. Jus' lemme know what Ah kin do for yo' to-night. That 'ere lobstuh Newburg's jus' about prime fo' eatin' this very minute, ef yo' feel a bit peckish."

"I do," P. Sybarite admitted. "Just a spoonful—"

"An' uh lil drink, suh? Jus' one lil innercent cocktail to fix yo' mouf right?"

"If you insist, Pete—if you insist."

"Yas-suh; and wif the lobstuh, suh, Ah venture to sug-gest a nice cold lil ha'f-pint of Cliquot, Yallah Label? How that strike yo' fancy, suh? Er mebbe yo'd perfuh—"

"Enough!" said P. Sybarite firmly. "A mere bite and a glass are enough to sustain life."

"Ain't that the troof?"

Chuckling, the negro waddled away, returned, and offered the guest a glass brimming with amber-tinted liquid.

Poising the vessel delicately between thumb and forefinger, P. Sybarite treated himself to one small sip—an instant of lingering delectation—another sip. So only, it is asserted, must the victim of the desert begin to allay his burning thirst; with discretion—a sip at a time—gingerly.

It was years since P. Sybarite had tasted a cocktail artfully concocted.

Dreamily he closed his eyes halfway. From a point in his anatomy a degree or two south of his diaphragm, a sensation of the most warm congratulation began to pervade his famished system: as if (he thought) his domestic economy were organising a torchlight procession by way of appropriate celebration.

Tender morsels of lobster smothered in cream and sherry (piping hot) daintiest possible wafers of bread-and-butter embracing leaves of pale lettuce, a hollow-stemmed glass effervescent with liquid sunlight of a most excellent bouquet, and then another: these served not in the least to subdue his occult jubilation.

Finally "the house," through the medium of its servitor, insisted that he top off with a cigar.

Ten years since his teeth had gripped a Fancy Tales of Smoke!...

Now it mustn't be understood that P. Sybarite entertained any misapprehensions as to the nature of the institution into which he had stumbled. He had not needed the sound, sometimes in quieter moments audible from upstairs, of a prolonged whirr ending in several staccato clicks, to make him shrewdly cognisant of its questionable character.

So at length, satiate and a little weary—drawn by curiosity besides—he rose, endowed Pete lavishly with a handful of small change (something over fifty cents; all he had in the world aside from his cherished five dollars), and with an impressive air of the most thorough-paced sophistication (nodding genially to the doorkeeper *en passant*) slowly ascended to the second floor.

Here, in remodelling the house for its present purposes, partitions had arbitrarily been dispensed with, aside from that enclosing the well of the stairway; the floor was one large room, wholly devoted to some half a dozen games of chance. With but few of these was P. Sybarite familiar; but on information and belief he marked down a faro layout, the device with which his reading had made him acquainted under the designation of *les petits chevaux*, and at either end of the saloon, immense roulette tables.

Upon all the gaming tables massive electric domes concentrated their light. The walls, otherwise severely unadorned, were covered with lustrous golden fabric; the windows were invisible, cloaked in splendid golden hangings; the carpet, golden brown in tone, was of a velvet pile so heavy that it completely muffled the sound of footsteps. The room, indeed, was singularly quiet for one that harboured some two-score players in addition to a full corps of dealers, croupiers, watchers, and waiters. The almost incessant whine of racing ivory balls with their clattering over the metal compartments of the roulette wheels, clicking of chips, dispassionate voices of croupiers, and an occasional low-pitched comment on the part of one or another of the patrons, seemed only to lend emphasis to the hush.

The warmth of the room was noticeable....

A brief survey of the gathering convinced P. Sybarite that, barring the servants, he was a lonely exception to the rule of evening dress. But this discovery discomfited him not at all. The wine buzzing in his head, his demeanour, not to mince matters, rakehelly, with an eye alert for the man with the twisted mouth, negligent hands in his trouser pockets, teeth tight upon that admirable cigar, he strutted hither and yon, ostensibly as much in his native element as a press agent in a theatre lobby.

A few minutes sufficed to demonstrate that the owner of the abandoned hat was not among those present; which fact, coupled with the doorkeeper's averment that Mr. Bailey Penfield was out, persuaded P. Sybarite that this last was neither more nor less than the proprietor of the premises. But this conclusion perturbed, completely unsettling his conviction regarding the *soi-disant* Miss Lessing; he couldn't imagine either her or Miss Marian Blessington in any way involved with a common (or even a proper) gambler.

To feel obliged constantly to revise his hasty inferences, he considered tremendously tiresome. It left one all up in the air!

His tour ended at last in a pause by the roulette table at the rear of the room. Curious to watch the game in being, he lingered there, head cocked shrewdly on one shoulder, a speculative pensiveness informing his eyes, his interest plainly aloof and impersonal. This despite the fact that his emotions of intestinal felicity were momentarily becoming more intense: the torchlight procession was in full swing, leaving an enduring refulgence wherever it passed.

There were perhaps half a dozen players round the board—

four on one wing, two on the other. Of the latter, one was that very young man who had been responsible for P. Sybarite's change of mind with regard to going home. With a bored air this prodigal was frittering away five-dollar notes on the colours, the columns, and the dozens: his ill success stupendous, his apparent indifference positively magnificent. But in the course of the little while that P. Sybarite watched, he either grew weary or succeeded in emptying his pockets, and ceasing to play, sat back with a grunt of impatience more than of disgust.

The ball ran its course thrice before he moved. Then abruptly lifting his finger to the croupier: "Five on the red, Andy," said he.

"Five on the red," repeated the croupier; and set aside a chocolate-coloured chip in memorandum of the wager.

When the ball settled again to rest, the announcement was monotonously recited: "Nine, red, odd, first dozen." And the blase prodigal was presented with the chocolate-coloured token.

Carelessly he tossed it upon the red diamond. Black won. Unperturbed, he made a second oral bet, this time on black, and lost; increased his wager to ten dollars on black—and lost; made it twenty, shifted to red, and lost; dropped back to five-dollar bets for three turns of the wheel, and lost them all. Fifty dollars in debt to the house, he rose, nodded casually to the croupier, left the room.

In mingled envy and amazement P. Sybarite watched him go. Fancy losing three weeks' wages and a third of another week's without turning a hair! Fancy losing fifty dollars without being required to pay up!

"Looks easy," meditated P. Sybarite with a thrill of dreadful yearning....

At precisely that instant the torchlight procession penetrated a territory theretofore unaffected, which received it with open arms and tumultuous rejoicings and even went so far as to start up a couple of bonfires of its own and hang out several strings of Japanese lanterns. In the midst of a confusion of soaring skyrockets and Roman candles vomiting showers of scintillant golden sparks, P. Sybarite was shocked to hear his own voice.

"Five on the red," it said distinctly, with an effect of extravagant apathy.

A thought later he caught the croupier's eye and drove the wager home with a nod. His heart stopped beating.

Five dollars! All he had in the world!

The *whirr* of the deadly little ball in its ebony runway was like nothing less than the exultant shriek of a banshee. Instantaneously (as if an accident had happened in the power house) every light in his body went out and left it cold and dark and altogether dismayed.

The croupier began his chant: "Three, red——!"

P. Sybarite failed to hear the rest. All the lights were on again, full blast. The croupier tossed him a chocolate token. He was conscious that he touched it with numb and witless fingers, mechanically pushing it upon the red diamond.

Ensued another awful, soul-sickening minute of suspense....

"Twenty-five, red——!"

A second brown chip appeared magically on top of the first. P. Sybarite regarded both stupidly; afraid to touch them, his brain communicated to his hand the impulse to remove the chips ere it was too late, but the hand hung moveless in listless mutiny.

"Thirty-four red—!"

Two more chips were added to his stack.

And this time his brain sulked. If his body wouldn't heed its plain and sagacious admonition—very well!—it just wouldn't bother to signal any further advice.

But quite instinctively his hand moved out, tenderly embraced the four brown chips, and transferred them to the green area dominated by the black diamond.

"Twelve, black—!"

Forty dollars were represented in that stunted pillar of brown wafers! P. Sybarite experienced an effect of coming to his senses after an abbreviated and, to tell the truth, somewhat nightmarish nap. Aping the manner of one or two other players whom he had observed before this madness possessed him, he thrust the chips out of the charmed circle of chance, and nodded again (with what a seasoned air!) to the croupier.

"Cash or chips?" enquired that functionary.

"Oh—cash, thank you."

The chips gathered into the company of their brethren, two twenty-dollar bills replaced them.

Stuffing these into his pocket, P. Sybarite turned and strolled indifferently toward the door.

"Better leave while your luck holds," Intelligence counselled.

"Right you are," he admitted fairly. "I'll go home now before anybody gets this away from me."

"Sensible of you," Intelligence approved.

"Still," suggested the small but clear voice of Greed, "you've got your original five dollars yet to lose. Be a sport. Don't go without turning in a cent to the house. It wouldn't look pretty."

"There's something in that," admitted P. Sybarite again.

Nevertheless, he never quite understood how it was that his feet carried him to the other roulette table, at the end of the salon opposite that at which he had been playing; or how it was that his fingers produced and coolly handed over the board, one of the twenty-dollar notes rather than the modest five he had meant to risk.

"How many?" the new croupier asked pleasantly.

P. Sybarite pulled a doubtful mouth. Five dollars' worth was all he really wanted. What on earth would he do with all the chips twenty dollars would buy? He'd need a bushel measure!

Before he could make up his mind, however, exactly twenty white counters were meted out to him.

"What are these worth?" he demanded incredulously, dropping into a chair.

"One dollar each," he was informed.

"Indeed?" he replied, politely smothering a slight yawn.

But he conceived a new respect for those infatuated men who so recklessly peppered the lay-out with chips—singly and in little piles of five and ten—worth one-hundred cents each!

However, to save his face, he'd have to go through his twenty. But after that—exit!

He made this promise to himself.

Prying a single chip apart from its fellows, he tossed it heedlessly upon the numbered squares. It landed upon its rim, rolled toward the wheel, and fainted gracefully upon the green compartment numbered 00.

The croupier cocked an eyebrow at him, as if questioning his intention, at the instant the ivory ball began to sing its song of a single note. Abruptly it was chattering; in another instant it was still.

"Double O!" announced a voice.

A player next P. Sybarite swore soulfully.

Thirty-five white chips were stacked alongside the winning stake. With unbecoming haste P. Sybarite removed them.

"Well," he sighed privately, "there's one thing certain: this won't last. But I don't like to seem a piker. I'll just make sure of this one: it can't win. And at that, I'll be another fifteen dollars in."

Deliberately he shifted the nineteen remaining of his original stack to keep company with his winning chip on the Double O....

A minute or so later the man at his elbow said excitedly: "I'll be damned if it didn't repeat! Can you beat that—!"

P. Sybarite stared stupidly.

"How's that?" he said.

"Double O," the croupier answered: "the second time."

"This is becoming uncanny," P. Sybarite observed to himself; and—"Cash!" said he aloud with cold decision.

Seven new one-hundred dollar certificates were placed in his hand. In a daze he counted, folded, and pocketed them. While thus engaged he heard the ball spin again. His original twenty dollars remained upon the double naught. Ten turned up: his stake was gathered in.

"You've had enough," Intelligence advised.

"Perfectly true," P. Sybarite admitted.

This time his anatomy proved quite docile. He found himself at the foot of the steps, fatuously smiling at the doorkeeper.

"He ain't come in yet," said the latter; "but he's liable to be here any minute now."

"Oh, yes," said P. Sybarite brightly, after a brief pause—"Mr. Penfield, of course. Sorry I can't wait."

"Well, you'll want your hat before you go—won't you?"

Placing an incredulous hand upon the crown of his head, P. Sybarite realised that it was covered exclusively with hair.

"I must have put it down somewhere upstairs," he murmured in panic.

"Mebbe you left it with Pete before you went up."

"Perhaps I did."

Turning back to the lounge, he entered to find it deserted save for the somnolent old gentleman and the hospitable Pete, but for whom P. Sybarite would probably never have known the delirious joy of that internal celebration or found the courage to risk his first bet.

And suddenly the fifty-cent tip previously bestowed upon the servitor seemed, to one unexpectedly fallen heir to the princely fortune then in P. Sybarite's pockets, the very nadir of beggarliness.

"Pete," said he with owlish gravity, "I begin to see that I have done you an inexcusable injustice."

Giggling, the negro scratched his head.

"Well, suh," he admitted, "Ah finds that gemmun gen'ly does change they min's erbout me, aftuh they done cut er melon, like."

With the air of an emperor, P. Sybarite gave the negro a twenty-dollar bill.

"And now," he cut short a storm of thanks, "if you'll be good enough to give me just one more glass of champagne, I think I'll totter home."

"Yas-*suh!*"

In a twinkling a glass was in his hand. As if it were so much water—in short, indifferently—P. Sybarite tossed it off.

"And my hat."

"Yo' hat?" Pete iterated in surprise. "Yo' didn't leaf yo' hat wif me, suh; yo' done tek it wif yo' when yo' went upstahs."

"Oh," murmured P. Sybarite, dashed.

He turned to the door, hesitated, turned back, and solemnly sat himself down.

"Pete," said he, extending his right foot, "I wish you'd do something for me."

"Yas-suh!"

"Take off my shoe."

Staring with naif incredulity until assured of the gentleman's complete seriousness, the negro plumped down upon his knees, unlaced, and removed the shoe.

"It's a shocking shoe," observed P. Sybarite dreamily.

Bending forward he tucked his original five-dollar note into the toe of the despised footgear.

"I am not going home broke," he explained laboriously to Pete; "as I certainly shall if I dare go upstairs again to find my hat."

"Yo's sholly sens'ble," Pete approved. "But they ain't no reason why yo' sho'd tek enny mo' chances ef yo' don't wantuh," he added, knotting the laces. "I'd just as leave's not go fetch yo' hat."

"You needn't bother," P. Sybarite returned with dignity.

IX

THE PLUNGER

A humour the most cool and reckless imaginable now possessed P. Sybarite. The first flush of his unaccustomed libations seemed to have worn itself out, his more recent draught to have had no other effect than to steady his gratulate senses; and a certain solid comfort resided in the knowledge that his hard-earned five dollars reposed in safe deposit.

"They can't get *that* away from me—not so long as I'm able to kick," he reflected with huge satisfaction.

And the seven hundred and thirty-five in his pocket was possessed of a devil of restlessness. He could almost feel it quivering with impatience to get into action. After all, it was only seven hundred and thirty-five dollars: not a cent more than the wages of forty-nine weeks' servitude to the Genius of the Vault of the Smell!

"That," mused P. Sybarite scornfully, "won't take me far...."

"What," he argued, "is the use of travelling if you can't go to the end of the line?..."

"I might as well be broke," he asseverated, "as the way I am!"

Glancing cunningly down his nose, he saw the finish of a fool.

"Anyway," he insisted, "it was ever my fondest ambition to get rid of precisely seven hundred and thirty-five dollars in one hour by the clock."

So he sat down at the end of the table of his first winnings, and exchanged one of his seven big bills for one hundred white chips.

"What," he asked with an ingenious smile, "is the maximum?"

"Seein's it's you," said the croupier, grinning, "we'll make it twenty a throw."

"Such being the case"—P. Sybarite pushed back the little army of white chips—"you may give me twenty dark-brown counters for these...."

In ten minutes he had lost two hundred dollars.

At the end of twenty minutes, he exchanged his last thirty-five dollars for seven brown chips.

Ten minutes later, he was worth eighteen hundred dollars; in another ten, he had before him counters calling for five thousand or thereabouts.

"It is," he observed privately—"it must be my Day of Days!"

A hand touched his shoulder, and a quiet voice said: "Beg pardon—"

He looked up with a slight start—that wasn't one of joyous welcome, because the speaker was altogether a stranger—to find at his elbow a large body of man entirely surrounded by evening clothes and urbanity; whose face was broad with plump cheeks particularly clean-shaven; whose eyes were keen and small and twinkling; whose fat hand (offered to P. Sybarite) was strikingly white and dimpled and well-manicured; whose dignity and poise (alike inimitable) combined with the complaisance of a seasoned student of mankind to mark an individuality at once insinuating and forceful.

"You were asking for me, I believe?" pursued this person, with complete suavity.

P. Sybarite pursed doubtful lips. "I'm afraid," he replied pleasantly, "you have the advantage of me.... Let's see: this is my thirty-second birthday...."

The ball was spinning. He deposited four chips on the square numbered 32.

"I am Mr. Penfield," the stranger explained.

"Really?" P. Sybarite jumped up and cordially seized his hand. "I hope I see you well to-night."

Releasing the hand, he sat down.

"Quite well, thank you; in fact, never better." With a slight smile Mr. Penfield nodded toward the gaming table. "Having a good time?"

"*Thirty-two, red, even,*" observed the croupier....

"Oh, tolerable, tolerable," assented P. Sybarite, blandly accepting counters that called for seven hundred dollars....

"In one year from to-day, I shall be thirty-three," he reckoned; and shifted a maximum to the square designated by that number....

"What do you think? Is Teddy going to get the nomination?"

"I'm only very slightly interested in politics," returned Mr. Penfield. "I shouldn't like to express an opinion.... Sorry a prior engagement obliged me to keep you waiting."

"*Thirty-three, black, odd....*"

"Don't mention it," insisted P. Sybarite politely. "Not another word of apology—I protest! Indeed, I've managed to divert myself amazingly while waiting.... Thank you," he added in acknowledgment of another seven-hundred-dollar consignment of chips. "To-day," he mused aloud, "is the thirteenth of April—"

"The fourteenth," corrected Mr. Penfield: "to-day is only about two hours old."

"Right you are," admitted P. Sybarite, shifting twenty dollars from the 13 to the 14. "Careless memory of mine ..."

"*Thirteen, black, odd....*"

"There, now! You see—you spoiled my aim," P. Sybarite complained peevishly.

"Forgive me," murmured Mr. Penfield while P. Sybarite made another wager. "Are you in a hurry to break the bank?" he added.

"It's my ambition," modestly confessed the little man, watching a second twenty gathered in to the benefit of the house. "But I've only a few minutes more—and you do play such a *darned* small game."

"Perhaps I can arrange matters for you," suggested Mr. Penfield. "You'd like the limit removed?"

"Not as bad as all that. Make the maximum a hundred, and I'll begin to feel at home."

"Delighted to oblige. You won't object to my rolling for you?" Penfield nodded to the croupier; who (first paying P. Sybarite seven hundred on his last wager) surrendered his place.

"Not in the least," agreed P. Sybarite, marshalling his chips in stacks of five: twenty-five dollars each. "It's an honour," he added, covering several numbers as Penfield deftly set ball and wheel in motion.

He won the first fall; and encouraged by this, began to play extravagantly, sowing the board liberally with wagers of twenty-five, fifty, and one hundred dollars each. Hardly ever the ball clattered to a lodgment but he cashed one or another of these; and the number of times that the house paid him thirty-five hundred dollars passed his count. All other play at that table ceased; and a gallery of patrons of the establishment gathered round, following with breathless interest the fortunes of this shabby little plunger. Their presence, far from annoying, pleased him; it was just so much additional assurance of fair play. The mounting of the roulette wheel—it was placed upon a broad sheet of plate-glass elevated several inches above the table—was proof against secret manipulation. And a throng of spectators not only forbade any attempt to call wrong numbers on a winning cast but likewise insured fair dealing on the part of the croupier, who was so busy raking in losing bets or paying winnings that P. Sybarite had time neither to watch him nor to check his payments.

Penfield, cool and smiling, confined his attention to the wheel. If he felt any uneasiness or dismay on account of P. Sybarite's steadily augmented mountain of chips, he betrayed it not at all overtly.

But abruptly (they had been playing less than fifteen minutes) he paused and, instead of starting the ball on another race round its ebony run, dropped it lightly in the depression immediately above the axle of the wheel.

"The game is closed," he announced evenly, with a slow smile. "Sir"—directly to P. Sybarite—"although it lacks the resources of Monte Carlo, this establishment nevertheless imitates its protective measures. A table losing twenty-five thousand dollars in one day ceases operations. You are just twenty-five thousand to the good. Accept my congratulations."

"You are very amiable," insisted P. Sybarite, rising, with a little bow. "But if you care for revenge, I shall be pleased to continue at the other table."

"Unfortunately that, too, has suspended operations," returned Penfield. "However, I hope before long to relieve you of your gains."

Opening the cash drawer, he cleared it completely of its contents, placing before P. Sybarite a tremendous accumulation of bills, old and new, of all denominations, loose and in packages, together with some ten or twelve golden double-eagles.

"I believe you will find that correct," he observed genially. "Afterwards, I trust you will do me the honour of splitting a bottle with me in the lounge."

"Delighted," said P. Sybarite.

Penfield strolled off, exchanged a few words with an acquaintance or two, and a few more with his employees, and went downstairs. The remaining handful of patrons disappeared gradually, yet so quickly that P. Sybarite was a lonely outsider by the time he had finished counting his winnings and stowing them away about his person.

Presenting the croupier with five hundred dollars, he recovered his hat (at last) and descended, to find Penfield awaiting him at the foot of the steps.

X

UNDER FIRE

Bloated though he was with lawless wealth and fat with insufferable self-satisfaction, P. Sybarite, trotting by the side of his host, was dwarfed alike in dignity and in physique, strongly resembling an especially cocky and ragged Airedale being tolerated by a well-groomed St. Bernard.

Now when Pete had placed a plate of caviare sandwiches between them, and filled their glasses from a newly opened bottle, he withdrew from the lounge and closed the door behind him; whether or not at a sign from Penfield, P. Sybarite was unaware; though as soon as they were alone and private, he grew unpleasantly sensitive to a drop in the temperature of the entente cordiale which had thus far obtained between himself and the gambler. Penfield's eyes promptly lost much of their genial glow, and simultaneously his face seemed weirdly less plump and rosy with prosperity and contentment. Notwithstanding this, with no loss of manner, he lifted a ceremonious glass to the health of his guest.

"Congratulations!" said he; and drank as a thirsty man drinks.

"May your shadow never grow less!" P. Sybarite returned, putting down an empty glass.

"That's a perfectly good wish plumb wasted," said Penfield, refilling both glasses, his features twisted in the wriest of grimaces. "Fact is—I don't mind telling you—your luck to-night has, I'm afraid, played the very devil with me. This house won't open up again until I raise another bank-roll."

"My sympathy," said P. Sybarite, sipping. "I'm really distressed.... And yet," he added thoughtfully, "you had no chance—none whatever."

"How's that?" said Penfield, staring.

"You couldn't have won against me to-night," P. Sybarite ingenuously explained; "it could *not* be done: I am invincible: it is—*Kismet!*—my Day of Days!"

Penfield laughed discordantly.

"Maybe it looks that way to you. But aren't you a little premature? You haven't banked that wad yet, you know. Any minute something might happen to make you think otherwise."

"Nothing like that is going to happen," P. Sybarite retorted with calm conviction. "The luck's with me at present!"

"And yet," said the other, abandoning his easy pose and sitting up with a sharpened glance and tone, "you are wrong—quite wrong."

"What makes you think that?" demanded P. Sybarite, finishing his second glass.

"Because," said his host with a dangerous smile, "I am a desperate man."

"Oh?" said P. Sybarite thoughtfully.

"Believe me," insisted the other with convincing simplicity: "I'm such a bum loser, I'm willing to stake my last five hundred on the proposition that you don't leave this house a dollar richer than you entered it."

"Done!" said P. Sybarite instantly. "If I get away with it, you pay me five hundred dollars. Is that right?"

"Exactly!"

"But—where shall we meet to settle the wager?"

Penfield smiled cheerfully. "Dine with me at the Bizarre this evening at seven."

"If I lose, with pleasure. Otherwise, you are to be my guest."

"It's a bargain."

"And—that being understood," pursued P. Sybarite curiously —"perhaps you won't mind explaining your grounds for this conspicuous confidence."

"Not in the least," said the other, pulling comfortably at his cigar—"that is, if you're willing to come through with a little information. I'm curious to know how you came to butt in here on my personal card of introduction. Where did you get it?"

"Found it in a hat left in my possession by a gentleman in a great hurry, whom I much desired to see again, and therefore —presuming him to be Mr. Bailey Penfield—came here to find."

"A gentleman unknown to you?"

"Entirely: a tall young man with an ugly mouth; rather fancies himself, I should say: a bit of a bounder. You recognise this sketch?"

"Perhaps ..." Penfield murmured thoughtfully.

"His name?"

"Maybe he wouldn't thank me for telling you that."

"Very well. Now then: why and how are you going to separate me from my winnings?"

"By force," said Mr. Penfield with engaging candour. "It desolates me to descend to rough-neck methods, but I am a larger, stronger man than you, Mr.—"

"Sybarite," said the little man, flushing, "P.—by the grace of God!—Sybarite."

"Delighted to make your acquaintance, Mr. Sybarite.... But before we lose our tempers, what do you say to a fair proposition: leave me what you have won to-night, and I'll pay it back to the last cent with interest in less than six months."

P. Sybarite shook his head: "I'm sorry."

The dark blood surged into Penfield's cheeks. "You won't accept my word—?"

"I have every confidence in your professional honour," P. Sybarite replied blandly, "up to the certain point to which we have attained to-night. But the truth is—I need the money."

"You're unwise," said the other, and sighed profoundly. "I'm sorry. You oblige me to go the extreme limit."

"Not I. On the contrary, I advise you against any such dangerous course."

"Dangerous?"

"If you interfere with me, I'll go to the police."

"The police?" Penfield elaborated an inflexion of derision. "I keep this precinct in my vest pocket."

"Possibly—so far as concerns your maintenance of a gambling house. But murder—that's another matter."

"Meaning, you refuse to submit without extreme measures?"

"Meaning just that, sir!"

Again the gambler sighed. "What must be, must," said he, rising. Moving to the wall, he pressed a call-button, and simultaneously whipped a revolver into view. "I hope you're not armed," he protested sincerely. "It would only make things messy. And then I hate to have my employees run any risk—"

"You are summoning a posse, I take it?" enquired P. Sybarite, likewise on his feet.

"Half a dozen huskies," assented the other. "If you know your little book, you'll come through at once and save yourself a manhandling."

"It's too bad," P. Sybarite regretted pensively—and cast a desperate glance round the room.

What he saw afforded him no comfort. The one door was unquestionably guarded on the farther side. The windows, though curtained, were as indubitably locked and further protected by steel outside blinds. Besides, Penfield bulked big and near at hand, a weapon of the most deadly calibre steadily levelled at the head of his guest.

But exactly at the moment when despair entered into the heart of the little man—dispossessing altogether his cool assumption of confidence in his star—there rang through the house a crash so heavy that its muffled thunder penetrated even the closed door of the lounge. Another followed it instantly, and at deliberate intervals a third and fourth.

Penfield blenched. His eyes wavered. He punched the bell-button a second time.

The door was thrown wide and—with the instantaneous effect of a jack-in-the-box—Pete showed a dirty-grey face of fright on the threshold.

"Good Lord, boss!" he yelled. "Run for yo' life! We's raided!"

He vanished....

With an oath, Penfield started toward the door—and instantly P. Sybarite shot at his gun hand like a terrier at the throat of a rat. Momentarily the shock of the assault staggered the gambler, and as he gave ground, reeling, P. Sybarite closed one set of sinewy fingers tight round his right wrist, and with the other seized and wrested the revolver away. The incident was history in a twinkling: P. Sybarite sprang back, armed, the situation reversed.

Recovering, Penfield threw him a cry of envenomed spite, and in one stride left the room. He was turning up the stairs, three steps and an oath at a bound, by the time P. Sybarite gained the threshold and sped his departing host with a reminder superfluously ironic:

"The Bizarre at seven—don't forget!"

A breathless imprecation dropped to him from the head of the staircase. And he chuckled—but cut the chuckle short when a heavy and metallic clang followed the disappearance of the gambler. The iron door upstairs had closed, shutting off the second floor from the lower part of the house, and at the same time consigning P. Sybarite to the mercies of the police as soon as they succeeded in battering down the front door.

Now he harboured no whim to figure as the sole victim of the raid—to be arrested as a common gambler, loaded to the guards with cash and unable to give any creditable account of himself.

"Damn!" said P. Sybarite thoughtfully.

The front doors still held, though shaking beneath a shower of axe-strokes that filled the house with sonorous echoes.

At his feet, immediately to the left of the lounge door, yawned the well of the basement stairway. And one chance was no more foolhardy than another. Like a shot down that dark hole he dropped—and brought up with a bang against a closed door at the bottom. Happily, it wasn't locked. Turning the handle, he stumbled through, reclosed the door, and intelligently bolted it.

He was now in a narrow and odorous corridor, running from front to rear of the basement. One or two doors open or ajar furnished all its light. Trying the first at a venture, P. Sybarite discovered what seemed a servant's bedroom, untenanted. The other introduced him to a kitchen of generous proportions and elaborate appointments—cool, airy, and aglow with glistening white paint and electric light; everything in absolute order with the exception of the central table, where sat a man asleep, head pillowed on arms folded amid a disorder of plates, bottles and glasses—asleep and snoring lustily.

P. Sybarite pulled up with a hand on the knob, and blinked with surprise—an emotion that would assuredly have been downright dismay had the sleeper been conscious. For he was in uniform; and a cap hung on the back of his chair; and uniform and cap alike boasted the insignia of the New York Police Department.

Wrinkling a perplexed nose, P. Sybarite swiftly considered the situation. Here was the policeman on the beat—one of those creatures of Penfield's vaunted vest-pocket crew—invited in for a bite and sup by the steward of the house. The steward called away, he had drifted naturally into a gentle nap. And now—"Glad I'm not in *his* shoes!" mused P. Sybarite.

And yet.... Urgent second thought changed the tenor of his temper toward the sleeper. Better far to be in his shoes than in those of P. Sybarite, just then....

Remembering Penfield's revolver, he made sure it was safe and handy in his pocket; then strode in and dropped an imperative hand on the policeman's shoulder.

"Here—wake up!" he cried; and shook him rudely.

The fellow stirred, grunted, and lifted a bemused, red countenance to the breaker of rest.

"Hello!" he said in dull perception of a stranger. "What's— row?"

"Get up—pull yourself together!" P. Sybarite ordered sternly. "You're liable to be broke for this!"

"Broke?" The officer's eyes widened, but remained cloudy with sleep, drink, and normal confusion. "Where's Jimmy? Who're you?"

"Never mind me. Look to yourself. This place is being raided."

"Raided!" The man leaped to his feet with a cry. "G'wan! It ain't possible!"

"Listen, if you don't believe me."

The crashing of the axes and the grumble of the curious crowd assembled in the street were distinctly audible. The officer needed no other confirmation; and yet—instant by instant it became more clearly apparent that he had drunk too deeply to be able to think for himself. Standing with a hand on the table, he rocked to and fro until, losing his balance, he sat down heavily.

"My Gawd!" he cried. "I'm done for!"

"Nonsense! No more than I—unless you're too big a fool to take a word of advice. Here—off with your coat."

"What's that?"

"I say, off with your coat, man—and look sharp! Get it off and I'll hide it while you slip into one of those waiter's jackets over there. Then, if they find us here, we can pretend to be employees. You understand?"

"We'll get pinched, all the same," the man objected stupidly.

"Well, if we do, it only means a trip to the Night Court, and a fine of five or ten dollars. You'll be up to-morrow for absence from post, of course, but that's better than being caught half-drunk in the basement of a gambling house on your beat."

Impressed, the officer started to unbutton his tunic, but hesitated.

"S'pose some of the boys recognise me?"

"Where are your wits?" demanded P. Sybarite in exasperation. "This isn't a precinct raid! You ought to know that. This is Whitman, going over everybody's head. Anyhow, it can't be worse for you than it is—and my way gives you a fighting chance to get off."

"Guess you're right," mumbled the other thickly, shrugging out of his coat and surrendering it.

Several white jackets hung from hooks on the wall near the door. Seizing one of these, the policeman had it on in a jiffy.

"Now what'll I do?" he pursued, as P. Sybarite, the blue coat over his arm, grabbed the police cap and started for the door.

"Do? How do I know? Use your own head for a while. Pull yourself together—cut some bread—do something useful—

make a noise like a steward—"

With this the little man shot out into the hallway, slammed the door behind him, and darted into the adjoining bedroom. Once there, he lost no time changing coats—not forgetting to shift his money as well—cocked the cap jauntily on one side of his head (a bit too big, it fitted better that way, anyhow) buttoned up, and left the room on the run. For by this time the front doors had fallen in and the upper floor was echoing with deep, excited voices and heavy, hurrying footsteps. In another moment or so they would be drawing the basement for fugitives.

He had planned—vaguely, inconclusively—to leave by the area door when the raiders turned their attention to the basement, presenting himself to the crowd in the street in the guise of an officer, and so make off. But now—with his fingers on the bolts—misgivings assailed him. He was physically not much like any policeman he had ever seen; and the blue tunic with its brass buttons was a wretched misfit on his slight body. He doubted whether his disguise would pass unchallenged— doubted so strongly that he doubled suddenly to the back door, flung it open, and threw himself out into the black strangeness of the night—and at the same time into the arms of two burly plain-clothes men posted there to forestall precisely such an attempt at escape.

Strong arms clipping him, he struggled violently for an instant.

"Here!" a voice warned him roughly. "It ain't goin' to do you no good—"

Another interrupted with an accent of deep disgust, in patent recognition of his borrowed plumage: "Damned if it ain't a patrolman!"

"Why the hell didn't you say so?" demanded the first as P. Sybarite fell back, free.

"Didn't—have—time. Here—gimme a leg over this fence, will you?"

"What the devil—!"

"They've got a door through to the next house—getting out that way. That's what I'm after—to stop 'em. Shut up!" P. Sybarite insisted savagely—"and give me a leg."

"Oh, well!" said one of the plain-clothes men in a slightly mollified voice—"if that's the way of it—all right."

"Come along, then," brusquely insisted the impostor, leading the way to the eastern wall of boards enclosing the back yard.

Curiously complaisant for one of his breed, the detective bent his back and made a stirrup of his clasped hands, but no sooner had P. Sybarite fitted foot to that same than the man started and, straightening up abruptly, threw him flat on his back.

"Patrolman, hell! Whatcha doin' in them pants and shoes if you're a patrol—"

"Hel-*lo*!" exclaimed the other indignantly. "Impersonatin' an officer—eh?"

With this he dived at P. Sybarite; who, having bounced up from a supine to a sitting position, promptly and peevishly swore, rolled to one side (barely eluding clutches that meant to him all those frightful and humiliating consequences that arrest means to the average man) and scrambled to his feet.

Immediately the others closed in upon him, supremely confident of overcoming by concerted action that smallish, pale, and terrified body. Whereupon P. Sybarite' stepped quickly to one side and, avoiding the rush of one, directly engaged the other. Ducking beneath a windmill play of arms, he shot an accurate fist at this aggressor's jaw; there was a click

Louis Joseph Vance

of teeth, the man's head snapped back, and folding up like a tripod, he subsided at length.

Then swinging on a heel, P. Sybarite met a second onset made more dangerous by the cooler calculations of a more sophisticated antagonist. Nevertheless, deftly blocking a rain of blows, he closed in as if eager to escape punishment, and planted a lifted knee in the large of the detective's stomach so neatly that he, too, collapsed like a punctured presidential boom and lay him down at rest.

Success so egregious momentarily stupefied even P. Sybarite. Gazing down upon those two still shapes, so mighty and formidable when sentient, he caught his breath in sharp amazement.

"Great Heavens! Is it possible *I* did that?" he cried aloud—and the next moment, spurred by alert discretion, was scaling the fence with the readiness of an alley-cat.

Instantaneously, as he poised above the abyss of Stygian blackness on the other side, not a little daunted by its imperturbable mystery, a quick backward glance showed him figures moving in the basement hallway of the gambling house; and easing over, he dropped.

Hard flags received him with native impassivity: stumbling, he lost balance and sat down with an emphasis that drove the breath from him in one mighty "*Ooof!*"

There was a simultaneous confusion of new, strange voices on the other side of the fence; cries of surprise, recognition, excitement:

"Feeny, by all that's holy!"

"Mike Grogan, or I'm a liar!"

"What hit the two av urn?"

"Gawd knows!"

"Thin 'tis this waay thim murdherous divvles is b'atin' ut!"

"Gimme a back up that fince!..."

P. Sybarite picked himself up with even more alacrity that if he'd landed in a bed of nettles, tore across that terra-incognita, found a second fence, and was beyond it in a twinkling.

Swift as he was, however, detection attended him—a voice roaring: "There goes wan av thim now!"

Other voices chimed in spendthrift with suggestions and advice....

Blindly clearing fence after fence without even thinking to count them, P. Sybarite hurtled onward. Noises in the rear indicated a determined pursuit: once a voice whooped—"*Halt or I fire!*"—and a shot, waking echoes, sped the fugitive's heels....

But in time he had of necessity to pause for breath, and pulled up in the back-yard of a Forty-sixth Street residence, his duty—to find a way to the street and a shift from that uniform of unhappy inspiration—as plain as the problem it presented was obscure.

Louis Joseph Vance

XI

BURGLARY UNDER ARMS

And there P. Sybarite stood, near the middle of a fence-enclosed area of earth and flagstones; winded and weary; looking up and all around him in distressed perplexity; in a stolen coat (to be honest about it) and with six months' income from a million dollars unlawfully procured and secreted upon his person; wanted for resisting arrest and assaulting the minions of the law; hounded by a vengeful and determined posse; unacquainted with his whereabouts, ignorant of any way of escape from that hollow square, round whose sides window after excitable window was lighting up in his honour; all in all, as distressful a figure of a fugitive from justice as ever was on land or sea....

Conceiving the block as a well a-brim with blackness and clamorous with violent sound, studded on high with inaccessible, yellow-bright loopholes wherefrom hostile eyes spied upon his every secret movement, and haunted below by vicious perils both animate and still: he found himself possessed of an overpowering desire to go away from there quickly.

But—short of further dabbling in crime—*how*?

To break his way to the street through one of those houses would he not only to invite apprehension: it would be downright burglary.

To continue his headlong career of the fugitive backyards tom-cat was out of the question, entirely too much like hard work, painful into the bargain—witness scratched and abraded palms and agonised shins. Sooner or later his strength must fail, some one would surely espy him and cry on the chase, he must be surrounded and overwhelmed: while to hide behind some ash-barrel was not only ignoble but downright fatuous: faith the most sublime in his *Kismet* couldn't excuse any hope that, eventually, he wouldn't be discovered and ignominiously routed out.

Very well, then! So be it! Calmly P. Sybarite elected to venture another and deeper dive into amateurish malfeasance; and gravely he studied the inoffensive building whose back premises he was then infesting.

It seemed to offer at least the negative invitation of desuetude. It showed no lights; had not an open window—so far as could be determined by straining sight aided only by a faint reflection from the livid skies. One felt warranted in assuming the premises to be vacant. Encouraging surmise! If such were in fact the case, he might hope soon to be counting his spoils in the privacy of his top-floor-hall-bedroom, back....

At the same time, to one ignorant of the primary principles of house-breaking, the problem of negotiating an entrance was of formidable proportions.

To break a basement window was feasible, certainly—but highly inadvisable for a number of obvious reasons.

To force a window-latch required (if memory served) a long flat-bladed knife—a kitchen knife; and P. Sybarite happened to have no such implement about him.

Similarly, to pry open the back door would require the services of a jimmy (whatever that might be).

Moreover, there were such things as burglar alarms—

inventions of the devil!

On the other hand, unless his senses deceived him, there were police officers in plenty only a fence or two away; and the back of this house boasted a fire-escape. By inverting a convenient ash-can and standing on it, an active man might possibly, if sufficiently desperate, manage to jump a vertical yard (more or less), catch the lowermost grating of the fire-escape, and draw himself up.

In a thought P. Sybarite turned the galvanised iron cylinder bottom-up, clambered upon it, and on tiptoe sought to gauge the exact distance of the requisite leap. But now the grating seemed to have receded at least three feet from its position as first judged—to be hopelessly removed from the grasp of his yearning fingers.

Yet that mad attempt must be made. Why die fighting when a broken neck would serve as well?

Gathering his slight person together, P. Sybarite crouched, quivered, jumped for glory and the Saints—and all but brained himself on that impish and trickish grating. Clutching it and kicking footloose, he was stunned by the wonder of many brilliant new-born constellations swirling round his poor head to the thunderous music of the spheres, as rendered by the ash-can which, displaced by the vigour of his acrobatics, had toppled over and was rolling and clattering hideously on the flagging.

In his terrified bosom P. Sybarite felt the heart of him turn to cold and clammy stone.

No clamour more infernal could well have been improvised, given similar circumstances and facilities as rude. It seemed hours, rather than instants, that the damned thing wallowed and bellowed beneath him, raising a din to disturb all Christendom. While, the moment it was still, the cries of the police pack belled clear and near at hand:

"This way, b'ys!"

"There he is, the—"

"Got 'im now—"

"Halt or—!"

Another pistol shot!...

Glancing over shoulder, the hunted man caught a glimpse of uncouth shapes wriggling along a fence ridge several rods away. No more than the barest glimpse, it served: with a mighty heave and wriggle he breasted the lower platform, shifted a hand to the top of its railing, heaved himself up to a foothold, and swarmed up the iron ladder with an agility an ape might have envied.

But as he mounted, it grew momentarily more evident that the stage thunder manufactured by that wretched galvanised iron cylinder had, in fact, served him far from ill; reverberating from wall to wall within the hollow of the block, its dozen echoes diverted pursuit to as many quarters, luring the limbs of the law every way but the right one. Nobody, it appeared, was alert enough to espy that fugacious shadow on the fire-ladder. And in less than a brace of minutes P. Sybarite, at the top, was pulling himself gingerly over the lip of a stone coping.

Surmising that he had gained not the roof of the house but that of a two-story rear extension, he found himself in what seemed a small roof-garden, made private by awnings and Venetian blinds. Between his soles and the stone flooring he could feel the yielding texture of a grass mat, and he could not only dimly discern but also smell the perfume of green things in pots here and there. And his first step forward brought him into soft collision with a wicker basket-chair.

He paused and took thought in perturbation.

Louis Joseph Vance

A most disappointing and deceptive sort of a house—inhabited, after all: its sombre and quiet aspect masking Heaven alone knew what pitfalls!...

Not a glint of light, not a sound....

When he moved again, it was with scrupulous caution.

Stealing softly on, the darkness seemed to thicken round him. He was sensible of suspense and qualms, of creeping flesh and an almost irresistible inclination to hold his breath. Uncanny business, this—penetrating unknown fastnesses of a dark and silent house at dead of night: a trespasser unable to surmise when the righteous householder, lurking on familiar ground and vigilant under arms, might not open fire....

Nevertheless, the police behind him were a menace of known calibre. With whatever shrinkings and dire misgivings, P. Sybarite went on.

Without misadventure he gained the main wall of the house, and there found open windows and (upon further cautious investigation) a doorway, likewise wide to the bland night air. Hesitant on the threshold of this last he sought with impotent senses to probe impenetrable obscurity—listening, every nerve taut and vibrant, for some sound significant of human tenancy, and detecting never an one. In spite of this, it was without the least confidence that presently he plucked up heart to proceed....

Three steps on into darkness, and his knee found a chair that might have poised itself on one leg, in malicious ambush, so promptly did it go over—and with what a racket.

Incontinently something rustled quite near at hand; followed a click—blinding light—a shrill, excited voice:

"Hands up!"

With a jerk, up went his hands high above his head. Blinking furiously in the glare, he comprehended his plight.

The lights he found so dazzling blazed from sconces round the walls of a bedroom more handsome than any he had thought ever to see—unless perhaps upon a stage. The voice belonged to a young woman sitting up in bed and coolly covering him with the yawning muzzle of a peculiarly poisonous-looking automatic pistol.

It was astonishingly evident that she wasn't at all frightened. The arm that levelled the weapon (a round and shapely arm, bare to the shoulder) was admirably steady; the rich colouring of her distinctly handsome face showed not a trace of pallor; and the fire that flickered in her large and darkly beautiful eyes was of indignation rather than of fear.

Abruptly she dropped her weapon and sat up yet straighter in her huddled bed-clothing, mouth and eyes widening with astonishment.

"Well!" she said quite simply—"I'll be damned if it ain't a cop!"

P. Sybarite immediately took occasion to lower his hands to a more comfortable position.

Fright inspired his latent histrionic genius; momentarily he became almost a good actor.

"Thank God!" he exclaimed fervently. "You're the one woman in a thousand who knows enough to look before she shoots! *Phwew!*'

Quite naturally he drew a braided blue cuff across a beaded forehead.

"That's all very well," the woman took him up sharply—"but be careful I don't shoot after looking. Cop or no cop, you—

what the devil do you want in my bedroom at this hour of the night?"

"Madam," P. Sybarite expostulated, aggrieved yet with an air of the utmost candour—"my duty, of course!"

"Duty!" she echoed. "What do you think you mean by that?"

"Perhaps," he countered blandly, "you're not aware a burglar has passed through this room?"

"A burglar? What rot!"

"Pardon me, madam," P. Sybarite lied nonchalantly, "but five minutes ago I was called in by the people in Two-thirty-three Forty-fifth Street, to nab a burglar who'd broken in there. They thought they had him locked up safe enough in one of the rooms, but when they came to open the door and let *me* at him—the bird had flown! He'd taken a long chance—swung himself from the window-ledge to a fire-escape five feet away—don't ask *me* how he did it! I got to the window just in time to see him go over the back fence. You heard me take a shot at him? No?"

"No, I didn't," said the woman in a manner eloquent of positive incredulity.

"Well, *any*way," P. Sybarite went on with elaborate ease, "I saw this man climb your fire-escape and so I came after him."

The woman frowned as she weighed this likely story; and P. Sybarite was at pains to conceal any exultation he may have felt over the prompt response of his vivid imagination to the call of exigence.

Would she or wouldn't she accept that wildly fanciful yarn of his? For moments that, brief though they must have been, seemed intolerably protracted, he awaited her verdict in the extremest anxiety—not, however, neglecting to employ the respite thus afforded him to make another quick survey of the room and a second and more shrewd appraisal of its admirably self-possessed tenant.

A bit too florid and ornate—he concluded—woman and lodgings alike were somewhat overdone. A superabundance of gilt and pink marred the colour scheme of the apartment; and there was ostentatious evidence of wealth lavishly expended on its furnishings. An overpowering voluptuousness of silken clothing dressed the bed itself.

But if her setting were luxurious, the woman outshone it tenfold with the dark splendour of her animal beauty. As comely and as able-bodied as a young pantheress, she was (one judged) little less dangerous—as vital, as self-centred, as deadly. Sitting up in bed, openly careless of charms hardly concealed by nightwear of sheer silk lace and *crepe de Chine*, she looked P. Sybarite up and down with wide eyes overwise in the ways of life, shrewdly judicious of mankind; handled her pistol with experienced confidence; spoke, in a voice of surpassing sweetness, with decision and considerable overt contempt for the phraseology of convention—swearing without the least affectation, slanging heartily when slang best suited her humour....

"Maybe you're telling the truth, at that," she announced suddenly, eyes coldly unprepossessed. "You sound fishy as all-hell, and God *knows* you're the sickest-looking cop I ever laid eyes on; but there are less unlikely things than that a second-story man should try this route for his getaway.... Well!" she demanded urgently—"what're you standing there for, like a stone man?"

"My dear lady—!" expostulated the dismayed P. Sybarite.

"Can the fond stuff and get busy. What're you going to do?"

"What am I—? What—ah—do you wish me to do?"

"If you're a cop, go to it—cop somebody," she replied with a brusque laugh—"and then clear out. I can use the room and time you're occupying. Besides, while you stand there staring as if you'd never seen a good-looking woman in a nightgown before, you're slipping the said burglar a fine young chance to make the front door—unless he's under the bed."

"Under the bed?" stammered the masquerader.

"You said something then," the woman snapped. "Why not look?"

Mechanically obedient to her suggestion, down P. Sybarite plumped on his knees, lifted the silken valance at the foot of the bed, and pretended to explore the darkness thereunder—finding precisely what he had anticipated, that is to say, nothing.

While thus occupied (and badgering his addled wits to invent some plausible way to elude this Amazon) he was at once startled and still further dismayed to hear the bed-springs creak, a light double thump as two bare feet found the floor, and again the woman's voice flavoured with acid sarcasm.

"You seem to find it interesting down there. Is it the view? Or are you trying to hypnotise your burglar by the well-known power of the human eye?"

"It's pure and simple reverence for the proprieties," P. Sybarite replied without stirring, "keeps me emulating the fatuous ostrich. I don't pretend it's comfortable, but I, believe me, madam, am a plain man, of modest tastes, unaccustomed to—"

"Get up!" the lady interrupted peremptorily. "I guess your regard for the proprieties won't suffer any more than my fair name. Come out of that and hunt burglars like a good little cop."

"But who am I," pleaded the little man, "to gaze unblinded

upon the sun?"

"That," said the lady, smothering a giggle, "will be about *all* from you. Get up—or I'll call in a sure-enough cop to search your title to that uniform."

Hastily P. Sybarite withdrew his head and rose. An embarrassed glance askance comforted him measurably: the lady had thrown an exquisite negligee over her nightdress and had thrust her pretty feet into extravagantly pretty silken mules.

"Now," said she tersely, "we'll comb the premises for this burglar of yours: and if we don't find him"—her lips tightened, her brows clouded ominously—"I promise you an interesting time of it!"

"I'm vastly diverted as it is—truly I am!" protested P. Sybarite, ruefully eyeing the lady's pistol. "But there's really no need to disturb yourself: I'm quite competent to take care of any housebreaker—"

"That," she broke in, "is something you'll have to show me.... Where's your nightstick?"

"My—er—what?"

"Your nightstick. What've you done with it?"

With consternation P. Sybarite investigated the vacant loop at his side.

"Must've dropped out while I was shinning over the back fence," he surmised vaguely. "However, I shan't need it. This"—with a bright and confident smile displaying Penfield's revolver—"will do just as well—better, in fact."

"That?" she questioned. "That's not a Police Department gun. Where'd you—"

"Oh, yes, it is. It's the new pattern—recently adopted. They've just begun to issue 'em. I got mine to-day—"

The lady's lips curled. "Very well," she concluded curtly. "I don't believe a word you say, but we'll see. Lead the way—show me one solitary sign that a burglar has been here—"

"Perhaps you'd prefer me to withdraw from the case?" the little man suggested with offended dignity. "After all, I may be mistaken—"

"You'd better not be. I warn you, find me a burglar—or"—she added with unmistakable significance—"I'll find one myself."

Interpreting the level challenge of her glance, P. Sybarite's heart quaked, his soul curdled, his stomach for picaresque adventure failed him entirely: anatomically, in short, he was hopelessly disqualified for his chosen role of favourite of *Kismet*, protagonist of this Day of Days. Withal, there was no use offering resistance to the demands of this masterful woman; she was patently one to be humoured against a more auspicious turn of affairs.

He shrugged, gave in with a gesture. Her imperative arm, uplifted, indicated an inner door.

"Find that burglar!"

"Swell chance I've got to get away with that proposition," he grumbled. "You've delayed me long enough to let any burglar get clean away!"

"And you hang back, giving him more time," she cut in. "Lead the way, now!"

Awed, P. Sybarite grasped his revolver and strode to the door with much dramatic manner, but paused with a hand on the knob to look over his shoulder.

The woman was there, not a foot distant, her countenance a mask of suspicious determination.

"Go on!" she commanded in menacing accents.

He pulled the door open, flung out into the hallway, paused again at the mouth of the back pit of the stairway.

Behind him the woman snapped a switch; an electric bulb glared out of the darkness. And P. Sybarite, peering down, started back with a gasp of amazement that was echoed in his ear.

On the stairs, halfway down, a man was crouching in a posture of frozen consternation: a small electric pocket-lamp burning brilliantly in one hand, the other, lifted, grasping a weapon of some curious sort, in the eyes of P. Sybarite more than anything else like, a small black cannon: a hatless man in evening clothes, his face half blotted out by a black mask that, enhancing the brightness of startled eyes gleaming through its peepholes, left uncovered only his angular muscular jaw and ugly, twisted mouth.

For a full minute (it seemed) not one of the three so much as drew breath; while through the haze of dumfounderment in P. Sybarite's brain there loomed the fact that once again *Kismet* had played into his hands to save his face in thus lending material body and substance to the burglar of his desperate invention.

And then, as if from a heart of agony, the woman at his side breathed a broken and tortured cry:

"You dog! So it's come to murder, has it?"

As if electrified by that ejaculation, P. Sybarite whipped up Penfield's revolver and levelled it at the man on the stairs.

"Hands up!" he snapped. "Drop that gun!"

The answer was a singular sound—half a choking cough, half a smothered bark—accompanied by a jet of fire from the strange weapon, and coincident with the tinkling of a splintered electric bulb.

Instantly the hall was again drenched in darkness but little mitigated by the light from the bedroom.

Heedless of consequences, in his excitement, P. Sybarite pulled trigger. The hammer fell on an empty chamber, rose and fell half a dozen times without educing any response other than the click of metal against metal: demonstrating beyond question that the revolver was unloaded.

From the hand of the marauder another tongue of flame licked out, to the sound of the same dull, bronchial cough; and a bullet thumped heavily into the wall beside P. Sybarite.

Enraged beyond measure, he drew back his worthless weapon and threw it with all his might. And *Kismet* winged the missile to the firing arm of the assassin. With a cry of pain and anger, this last involuntarily relaxed his grasp and, dropping his own pistol, stumbled and half fell, half threw himself down to the next floor.

As this happened, a white arm was levelled over the shoulder of P. Sybarite.

The woman took deliberate aim, fired—and missed.

XII

THE LADY OF THE HOUSE

Until that moment of the woman's shot, what with the failure of P. Sybarite's weapon to fire and the strange, muted coughing of the assassin's, an atmosphere of veritable decorum, nothing less, had seemed to mark the triangular duel, lending it something of the fantastic quality of a nightmare: an effect to which the discovery of a marauder, where P. Sybarite had expected to find nobody, added measurably....

But now, temporarily blinded by that vicious bright blade of flame stabbing the gloom a hand's breadth from his eyes, and deafened by the crash of the explosion not two feet from his ear-drums, he quickened to the circumstances with much of the confusion of a man awakened by a thunder-clap from evil dreams to realities yet more grim.

Of a sudden he understood that murder had been attempted in his presence and knowledge: a stark and hideous fact, jarring upon the semi-humorous indulgence with which hitherto he had been inclined to regard the unfolding of this night of *outre* adventure. Twice the man had shot to kill with that singular weapon of silent deadliness—and both times had missed his mark by the barest margin....

At once, like a demon of exceptional malignity, a breathless and overpowering rage possessed P. Sybarite. Without the least hesitation he stretched forth a hand, snatched the pistol from

Louis Joseph Vance

the grasp of the woman—who seemed to relinquish it more through surprise than willingly—threw himself halfway down the stairs, and took a hasty pot-shot at the man—almost invisible in the darkness as he rounded the turn of the next flight.

Missing, P. Sybarite flung on recklessly. As he gained the lower floor, the hall lights flashed up, switched on from the upper landing by the woman of the house. Thus aided, he caught another glimpse of his prey midway down the next flight, and checked to take a second shot.

Again he missed; and as the bullet buried itself in splintering wainscoting, a cry of almost childish petulence escaped him. With but one thought, he hurled on, swung round to the head of the stairs, saw his man at the bottom, pulled up to aim, and....

Beneath him a small rug slipped on polished parquetry of the landing. P. Sybarite's heels went up and his head down with a sickening thump. He heard his pistol explode once more, and again visioned a reeling firmament fugitively coruscant with strange constellations.

Then—bounding up with uncommon resiliency—he saw the street door of the house close behind the fugitive and heard the heavy slam of it.

In another breath, pulling himself together, he was up and descending three and four steps at a stride. Reaching the door, he threw it open and himself heedlessly out and down a high stone stoop to the sidewalk—pulled up, bewildered to discover himself the sole living thing visible in all that night-hushed stretch between Fifth Avenue and Sixth: of the assassin there was neither sign nor sound....

He felt perilously on the verge of tears—would gladly have bawled and howled with temper—and gained little relief from another short-lived break of heartfelt profanity—something halting and inexpert, truth to tell.

Above him, on the stoop, the lady of the house appeared; paused to peer searchingly east and west; looked down at the trembling figure of the small man in his overgrown police tunic, shaking an impotent fist in the face of the City of New York; and laughed quietly to herself.

"Come back," she called in a guarded tone. "He's made a clean getaway. Got to hand him *that*. No use trying to follow—you'd never catch up in a thousand years. Come back—d'you hear?—and give me my gun!"

A trifle dashed, P. Sybarite raked the street with final reluctant glances; then in a spirit of witless and unquestioning docility returned.

The woman retired to the vestibule, where she closed and locked the door as he passed through, further ensuring security by means of a chain-bolt; then entering the hallway, closed, locked, and similarly bolted the inner doors.

"Now, then!" she addressed the little man with a brilliant smile—"now we can pow-wow. Come into the den"—and led the way toward the rear of the house.

Trotting submissively in her wake, his wrinkled nose and batting eyelids were eloquent of the dumb amaze with which he was reviewing this incredible affair.

Turning into a dark doorway, the woman switched light into an electric dome, illuminating an interior apartment transformed, by a wildly original taste in eccentric decoration, into a lounging room of such distressful uniquity that it would have bred unrest in the soul of a lotus-eater.

Black, red, and gold—lustreless black of coke, lurid crimson of fresh blood, bright glaring yellow of gold new-minted—were the predominant notes in a colour scheme at once sombre and violent. The walls were hung with scarlet tapestries whereon gold dragons crawled and fought or strove to swallow dead black planets, while on every hand black imps of Eblis writhed and struggled over golden screens, golden devils mocked and mowed from panels of cinnabar, and horrific masks of crimson lacquer, picked out with gold and black, leered and snarled dumb menaces from darkened corners.

In such a room as this the mildest mannered man, steeping his soul in the solace of mellow tobacco, might have been pardoned for dreaming lustfully of battle, murder and sudden death, or for contemplating with entire equanimity the tortured squirmings of some favourite enemy upon the rack.

"Cosy little hole," P. Sybarite couldn't forbear to comment with a shudder as he dropped into a chair in compliance with the woman's gesture.

"I have my whims," she said. "How would you like a drink?"

"Not at all," he insisted hastily. "I've had all I need for the time being."

"That's a mercy," she replied. "I don't much feel like waiting on you myself, and the servants are all abed."

Offering cigarettes in a golden casket, she selected and lighted one for herself.

"You have servants in the house, then?"

"Do I look like a woman who does her own housework?"

"You do not," he affirmed politely. "But can you blame me for wondering where your servants've been all through this racket?"

"They sleep on the top floor, behind sound-proof doors," his hostess explained complacently, "and have orders to answer only when I ring, even if they should happen to hear anything. I've a passion for privacy in my own home—another whim, if you like."

"It's nothing to me, I assure you," he protested. "Minding my own business is one of the best little things I do."

"If that's so, why do you walk uninvited into strange bedrooms at all hours, pretending to be a policeman, with a cock-and-bull yarn about a burglar—"

"But there was a burglar!" P. Sybarite contended brightly. "You saw him yourself."

"No."

"But—but you *did* see him—later, on the stairs!"

Smiling, the woman shook her head. "I saw no burglar—merely a dear friend. In short, if it interests you to know, I saw my husband."

"Madam!" P. Sybarite sat up with a shocked expression.

"Oh," said the woman lightly, "we're good enough for one another—he and I. He deserved what he got when he married me. But that's not saying I'm content to see him duck what's coming to him for to-night's deviltry. In fact, I mean to get him before he gets me. Are you game to lend me a hand?"

"Me, madam!" cried P. Sybarite in alarm. "Far be it from me to come between husband and wife!"

"Don't be afraid: I'm not asking you to dabble your innocent hands in a fellow-human's blood—merely to run an errand for me."

"Really—I'd rather be excused."

"Really," she mocked pleasantly, "you won't be. I'm a gentle creature but determined—frail but firm, you know. Perhaps you've heard of me—Mrs. Jefferson Inche?"

Decidedly he had; and so had nine-tenths of New York's newspaper-reading population. His eyes widened with new interest.

"Truly?" he said, civilly responsive to the challenge in her announcement. "But *I* never knew Mrs. Jefferson Inche was beautiful."

"It needs a beautiful woman to be known as the most dangerous in Town," she explained with modest pride.

"But—ah—Mr. Inche, I understand, died some years ago."

"So he did."

"Yet you speak of your husband—?"

"Of my present husband, whose name I don't wear for reasons of real-estate. I took the rotter on because he's rich and will be richer when his father dies; he married me because he was rotten and I had the worst reputation he could discover. So we're quits *there*. If our marriage comes out prematurely, he'll be disinherited; so we've agreed to a *sub-rosa* arrangement which leaves him, ostensibly, a marketable bachelor. Now, I happen to know a marriage has recently been offered him through which he would immediately come into control of a big pot of money, and naturally he's strong for it. But I refused his offer of a cool half-million to play the Reno circuit, and so he concluded to sue for a divorce with a revolver, a Maxim silencer, and a perfect alibi. Do you follow me?"

"As far as the alibi."

"Oh, that's quite simple. We don't live together, and he's in sure-enough society, and I'm not. To-night the annual

Hadley-Owen post-lenten masquerade's in full swing just around the corner, and friend husband's there with the rest of the haughty bunch. Can't you see how easy it would be for him to drop round here between dances, murder his lawful wedded wife, and beat it back, without his absence ever being noticed?"

"It does sound feasible, if—ah—sickening," P. Sybarite admitted. "But really, it's hard to believe. Are you positive—?"

"I tell you," said the woman impatiently, "I recognised him; I saw his mouth—his mask wouldn't hide that—and knew him instantly."

P. Sybarite was silent: he, too, had recognized that mouth.

Briefly he meditated upon this curious freak of *Kismet* that was linking his fortunes of the night with those of the man with the twisted mouth.

"Now you know the lay of the land—how about helping me out?"

Now the trail of the man with the twisted mouth promised fair to lead to Molly Lessing. P. Sybarite didn't linger on his decision.

"I'm awf'ly impressionable," he conceded with a sigh; "some day, I'm afraid, it'll get me in a peck of trouble."

"I can count on you, then?"

"Short of trying a 'prentice hand at assassination—"

"Don't be an ass. I only want to protect myself. Besides, you can't refuse. Consider how lenient I've been with you."

P. Sybarite lifted questioning eyebrows, and dragged down the corners of a dubious mouth.

"If I wanted to be nasty," Mrs. Inche explained, "you'd be on your way now to a cell in the East Fifty-first Street station. But I was grateful."

"The Saints be praised for that!" exclaimed the little man fervently. "What's it for?"

"For waking me up in time to prevent my murder in my sleep," she returned coolly; "and also for being the spunky little devil you are and chasing off that hound of a husband of mine. If it wasn't for you, he'd've got me sure. Or else," she amended, "I'd've got him; which would have been almost as unpleasant—what with being pinched and tried and having juries disagree and getting off at last only on the plea of insanity—and all that."

"Madam," said P. Sybarite, rising, "the more I see of you, the more you claim my admiration. I entreat you, permit me to go away before my emotion deepens into disastrous infatuation."

"Sit down," countered Mrs. Inche amiably; "don't be afraid—I don't bite. Now you know who I am, but before you go, I mean to know who you are."

"Michael Monahan, madam." This was the first alliterative combination to pop into his optimistic mind.

"Can that," retorted the lady serenely—"solder it up tight, along with the business of pretending to be a cop. It won't get you anything. I've a proposition to make to you."

"But, madam," he declared with his naif and disarming grin— "believe me—my young affections are already engaged."

"You're not half the imbecile you make yourself out," she judged soberly. "Come—what's your name?"

Taking thought, he saw no great danger in being truthful for once.

"P., unfortunately, Sybarite," he said: "bookkeeper for Whigham and Wimper—leather merchants, Frankfort Street."

"And how did you come by that coat and hat?"

"Borrowed it from a drunken cop in Penfield's, a little while ago. They were raiding the place and I kind of wanted to get away. Strange to say, my disguise didn't take, and I had to leave by way of the back fences in order to continue uninterrupted enjoyment of the inalienable rights of every American citizen—life, liberty, the pursuit of happiness."

"I don't know why I believe you," said Mrs. Inche reflectively, when he paused for breath. "Perhaps it's your spendthrift way with language. Do you talk like that when sober?"

"Judge for yourself."

"All right," she laughed indulgently: "I believe everything you say. Now what'll you take to do me a service?"

"My services, madam, are yours to command: my reward— ah—your smile."

"Bunk," observed the lady elegantly. "How would a hundred look to you? Good, eh?"

"You misjudge me," the little man insisted. "Money is really no object."

"Still"—she frowned in puzzlement—"I should think a clerk in the leather business—!"

"I'm afraid I've misled you. I should have said that I *was* a clerk in the leather business until to-day. Now I happen to be independently wealthy, a clerk no longer."

"How's that—wealthy?"

"Came into a small fortune this evening—nothing immodest, but ample for one of my simple tastes and modest ambitions."

"I think," announced the lady thoughtfully, "that you are one of the slickest young liars I ever listened to."

"That must be considerable eminence," considered P. Sybarite with humility.

"On the other hand, you're unquestionably a perfect little gentleman," she pursued. "And anyhow I'm going to take you at your word and trust you. If you ever change your mind about that hundred, all you've got to do is to come back and speak for it.... Do I make you right? You're willing to go a bit out of your way to do me a favour to-night?"

"Or any other night."

"Very well." Mrs. Inche rose. "Wait here a moment."

Wrapping her negligee round her, she swept magnificently out of the "den," and a moment later again crossed P. Sybarite's range of vision as she ascended the stairs. Then she disappeared, and there was silence in the house: a breathing spell which the little man strove to employ to the best advantage by endeavouring to assort and rearrange his sadly disordered impressions.

Aware that he would probably do wisely to rise and flee the place, he none the less lingered, vastly intrigued and more than half inclined to see the affair through to the end.

His confused reverie was presently interrupted by the sound of the woman's high, clear voice at a telephone located (he fancied) somewhere in the hallway of the second story.

"Hello! Columbus, seven, four hundred, please.... Hello— Mason?... Taxicab, please—Mrs. Jefferson Inche.... Yes— charge....

Yes—immediately.... Thank you!"

A moment later she reappeared on the stairs, carrying a wrap of some sort over her arm: a circumstance which caused P. Sybarite uneasily to wonder if she meant to push her notorious indifference to convention to the limit of going out in a taxicab with no other addition to her airy costume than a cloak.

But when she again entered the "den," it proved to be a man's coat and soft hat that she had found for him.

"Get up," she ordered imperiously, "and change to these before you get pinched for impersonating an officer. I've called a taxi for you, and this is what I want you to do: go to Dutch House—that's a dive on Fortieth Street—"

"I've heard of it," nodded P. Sybarite. "Any sober man who stays away from it is almost perfectly safe, I believe."

"I'll back you to take care of yourself," said the lady. "Ask for Red November.... You know who he is?"

"The gangster? Yes."

"If he isn't in, wait for him if you wait till daylight—"

"Important as all that, eh?"

"It's life or death to me," said Mrs. Inche serenely. "I've got to have protection—you've seen yourself how had I need it. And the police are not for the likes of me. Besides," she added with engaging candour, "if I squeal and tell the truth, then friend husband will be disinherited for sure, and I'll have had all my trouble for nothing."

"You make it perfectly clear, Mrs. Inche.... And when I see Mr. Red November—?"

"Say to him three words: *Nella wants you.* He'll understand. Then you can go home."

"*If* I get out alive."

"You're safe if you don't drink anything there."

"Doubtless; but I'll feel safer if you'll lend me the loan of this pretty toy," said P. Sybarite, weighing in one hand her automatic pistol.

"It's yours."

"Anything in it?"

"Three shots left, I believe. No matter. I'll get you a handful of cartridges and you can reload the clip in the taxicab. Not that you're likely to need it at Dutch House."

From the street rose the rumble of a motor, punctuated by a horn that honked.

"There's the cab, now," announced Mrs. Inche briskly. "Shake yourself out of that coat and into this—and hustle!"

"It's my impressionable nature makes all my troubles," observed P. Sybarite disconsolately. "However..."

Shrugging into the coat Mrs. Inche held for him, he cocked the felt hat jauntily on the side of his head.

"Always," he proclaimed with gesture—hand on heart— "always the ladies' slave!"

XIII

RESPECTABILITY

But when it came to viscid second thought, alone in the gloom of an unsympathetic taxicab, P. Sybarite inclined to concede himself more ass than hero. It was all very well to say that, having spread his sails to the winds of *Kismet*, he was bound to let himself drift to their vagrant humour: but there are certain channels of New York life into which even the most courageous mariner were ill-advised to adventure under pilotage no more trustworthy than that of sufficient champagne and a run of good luck.

Dutch House in Fortieth Street, West, wore the reputation of being as sinister a dive as ever stood cheek-by-jowl with Broadway and brazenly flaunted an all-night liquor license in the face of law-abiding New York; of which it was said that no sober man ever went there, other than those who went to prey, and that no drunkard ever escaped from it unfleeced; haunt of the most deadly riff-raff to be found in Town, barring inmates of certain negro stews on the lower West Side and of some of the dens to which the sightseer does *not* penetrate in the tour of Chinatown.

Grim stories were current of men who had wandered thither in their cups, "for the lark of it," only to return to consciousness days afterwards, stripped, shorn, and shattered in health bodily and mental, to find themselves in some vile kennel miles from Dutch House; and of other men who passed once through its foul portals and—passed out a secret way, never to return to the ken of their friends....

Yet it stood, and it stands, waxing fat in the folly of man and his greed.

And to this place P. Sybarite was travelling to deliver a message from a famous demi-rep to a notorious gang leader; with only a .25 calibre Colt's automatic and his native wit and audacity to guard the moderate fortune that he carried with him in cash—a single hundredth part of which would have been sufficient to purchase his obliteration at the hands of the crew that ran the place.

However, in their ignorance his safety inhered; and it was not really necessary that he advertise his swollen fortunes; and as for the gold in his trousers pocket—a ponderable weight, liable to chink treacherously when he moved—P. Sybarite removed this and thoughtfully cached it under one of the cushions of his cab. It seemed a long chance to take with a hundred dollars: but a hundred dollars wasn't a great deal, after all, to a man as flush as he; and better lose it all (said he) than make a noise like a peripatetic mint in a den of thieves and worse....

The cab drawing up to the curb, out P. Sybarite hopped, a dollar in hand for the chauffeur, and the admonition: "I'm keeping you; wait till I come out, if I'm all night; and don't let your motor die, 'cause I *may* be in a hurry."

"Gotcha," said the chauffeur tersely; pocketed the bill; lighted a cigarette....

P. Sybarite held back an instant to inspect the approach.

This being Sunday morning, Dutch House was decorously dull to the street; the doors to the bar closed, the lights within low and drowsy; even the side door, giving access to the "restaurant," was closed much of the time—when, that is to say, it wasn't swinging to admit an intermittent flow of belated casuals and habitues of both sexes.

A row of vehicles lined the curb: nighthawk taxicabs for the most part, with one or two four-wheelers, as many disreputable and dilapidated hansoms, and (aside from that in which P. Sybarite had arrived) a single taxicab of decent appearance. This last stood, with door ajar, immediately opposite the side entrance, its motor pulsing audibly—evidently waiting under orders similar to those issued by P. Sybarite.

Now as the latter advanced to enter Dutch House, shadows appeared on the ground glass of the side door; and opening with a jerk, it let out a gush of fetid air together with Respectability on the prowl—Respectability incognito, sly, furtive of air, and in noticeable haste.

He paused for a bare instant on the threshold; affording P. Sybarite opportunity for a good, long look.

"Two-thirty," said Respectability brusquely over his shoulder.

The man behind him growled affirmation: "Two-thirty—don't worry: I'll be on the job."

"And take care of that boy."

"Grab it from me, boss, when he wakes up, he won't know where he's been."

"Good-night, then," said Respectability grudgingly.

"G'd-night."

The door closed, and with an ineradicable manner of weight and consequence Respectability turned toward the waiting taxicab: a man of, say, well-preserved sixty, with a blowsy plump face and fat white side-whiskers, a fleshy nose and arrogant eyes, a double chin and a heavy paunch; one who, in brief, had no business in that galley at that or any other hour of day or night, and who knew it and knew that others (worse luck!) would know it at sight.

All this P. Sybarite comprehended in a glance and, comprehending, bristled like a truculent game-cock or the faithful hound in the ghost-story. The aspect of Respectability seemed to have upon him the effect of a violent irritant; his eyes took on a hot, hard look, his lips narrowed to a thin, inflexible crease, and his hands unconsciously closed.

And as Respectability strode across the sidewalk, obviously intending to bury himself in the body of his waiting cab as quickly as possible, P. Sybarite—with the impudence of a tug blocking the fairway for an ocean liner—stepped in his path, dropped a shoulder, and planted both feet firmly.

Immediately the two came together; the shoulder of P. Sybarite in the paunch of Respectability, evoking a deep grunt of choleric surprise and bringing the gentleman to an abrupt standstill.

Upon this, P. Sybarite's mouth relaxed; he smiled faintly, almost placatingly.

"Well, old top!" he cried with malicious cordiality. "Who'd think to meet *you* here! What's the matter? Has high finance turned too risky for your stomach? Or are you dabbling in low-life for the sheer fun of it—to titillate your jaded senses?"

Respectability's cheeks puffed out like red toy balloons; so likewise his chest.

"Sir!" he snorted—"you are drunk!"

"Sir!" retorted P. Sybarite, none too meekly—"you lie."

The ebony-and-gold cane of Respectability quivered in mid-air.

"Out of my way!"

"Put down that cane, Mr. Brian Shaynon," said P. Sybarite peaceably, "unless you want me to play horse with you in a way to let all New York know how you spend the wee sma' hours!"

At the mention of his name Respectability stiffened in dismay.

"Damnation!" he cried hoarsely. "Who are you?"

"Why, have you forgotten me? Careless of you, Mr. Shaynon. I'm the little guy that put the speck in Respectability: I'm the noisy little skeleton in the cupboard of your conscience. Don't you know me now?"

With a gasp (prudently lowering his stick) Mr. Shaynon bent to peer into the face exposed as P. Sybarite pushed back his hat; stared an instant, goggling; wheeled about, and flung heavily toward his taxicab.

"The Bizarre!" wheezed he to the chauffeur; and dodging in, banged the door.

As for P. Sybarite, he watched the vehicle swing away and round the corner of Seventh Avenue, a doubtful glimmer in eyes that had burned hot with hostility, a slight ironic smile wreathing lips that had shown hatred.

"But what's the good of that?" he said in self-disgust, as the taxicab disappeared.

With a sigh, shaking himself together, he went into Dutch House.

XIV

WHERE ANGELS FEAR TO TREAD

From street door to restaurant entrance, the hallway of Dutch House was some twenty-five feet long, floored with grimy linoleum in imitation of tiling, greasy as to its walls and ceiling, and boasting an atmosphere rank with a reek compounded of a dozen elements, in their number alcohol, cheap perfumery, cooked meats, the sweat of unclean humanity, and stale tobacco smoke.

Save for this unsavoury composite wraith, the hall was empty when P. Sybarite entered it. But it echoed with sounds of rowdy revelry from the room in back: mechanical clatter of galled and spavined piano, despondent growling of a broken-winded 'cello, nervous giggling and moaning of an excoriated violin—the three wringing from the score of *O You Beautiful Doll* an entirely adequate accompaniment to the perfunctory performance of a husky contralto.

Though by no means squeamish, on the testimony of his nose and ears P. Sybarite then and there concluded that he would have to have become exceedingly blase indeed to find Dutch House amusing.

And when he had gone on into the restaurant itself, slipping his modest person inconspicuously into a chair at the nearest unoccupied table, the testimony of his other senses as to the character of his company served to confirm this impression.

"It's no use," he sighed: "I'm too old a dog.... Be it ever so typical, there's *no* place like one's own hash-foundry." ...

This room was broad and deep, and boasted, at its far end, a miniature stage supporting the orchestra and, temporarily, the gyrations of a lady in a vivacious scarlet costume—mistress of the shopworn contralto—who was "vamping with the feet" the interval between two verses of her ballad.

The main floor was strewn with tables round which sat a motley gathering of gangsters, fools, pretty iniquities and others by no stretch of the imagination to be termed pretty, confidence men, gambling touts, and the sprinkling of drunkards—plain, common, transient, periodical, suburban, habitual, and unconscious—for and by whom the place was, and is, maintained. In and out among these circulated several able-bodied waiters with soiled shirt-bosoms, iron jaws and, not infrequently, cauliflower ears.

Spying out P. Sybarite, one of these bore down upon him with an air of the most flattering camaraderie.

It was true that the little man, in a dark coat and hat alike too large for him, with his shabby shoes and trousers and apologetic demeanour, promised no very profitable plucking; but the rule of Dutch House is to neglect none, however lowly.

"Well, bo'," grunted the waiter cheerfully, polishing off the top of the table with a saturated towel, "yuh don't come round's often as y' uster."

"That's a fact," P. Sybarite agreed. "I've been a long time away—haven't I?"

"Yuh said somethin' *then*. Mus' be months sinst I seen yuh last. What's the trouble? Y' ain't soured on the old joint, huh?"

"No," P. Sybarite apologised. "I've been—away. Where's Red?"

"MacManus—?" asked the waiter, beginning to believe that this strange little creature must in fact be a "regular" of the "bunch"—one whose name and face had somehow, unaccountably, slipped from his memory.

"November," P. Sybarite corrected.

"Oh, he's stickin' round—pretty busy to-night. Wouldn't fuss him, 'f I was yuh, 'less it's somethin' extra."

"I make you," said the little man. "But this is his business. Tell him I have a message for him, will you?"

"Just as yuh say, bo'," returned the other cautiously. "What's it goin' to be? Bucket of grape or a tub of suds?"

"Do I look like the foolish waters?" enquired P. Sybarite with mild resentment. "Back me up a shell of lather."

Grinning amiably at this happy metaphorical description of the glass of lager regularly served at Dutch House, the waiter shouldered through the swinging doors to the bar....

Then fell a brief lull in the melange of music and tongues, during which a boyish voice lifted up in clear remonstrance at a table some three removed from that at which P. Sybarite sat:

"But I don't *want* anything more to drink!"

P. Sybarite looked that way. The owner of the voice (now again drowned) was apparently a youngster of twenty years—not more—clean of limb and feature, with a hot flush discolouring his good-looking face, a hectic glitter in his eyes, and a stubborn smile on his lips.

Lounging low in a straight-backed chair, with his hands in his pockets and his head wagging obstinately, he was plainly intoxicated, but as yet at a stage sufficiently mild to admit of his recognising the self-evident truth that he needed not another drop.

Yet his companions would have him drink more deeply.

Of these, one was a woman of no uncertain caste, a woman handsome in a daring and costly gown, and as yet not old, but in whose eyes flickered a curious febrile glare ("as though," commented P. Sybarite, moralist, "reflected back from the mouth of Hell").

The other was a man singularly handsome in a foreign way—Italian, at an indifferent guess—slight and graceful of person in well-tailored if somewhat flashy clothing; boasting too much jewellery; his teeth gleaming a vivid white against his dark colouring as he smiled good-humouredly in his attempts to press more drink upon the other.

The music stopped altogether for a time, and again the boy's voice rang out clearly:

"Tell you—'ve had enough."

The Italian said something urgent, in an undertone. The woman added inaudible persuasion to his argument. The boy looked from one to another with a semi-stupid smile; but wagged an obdurate head.

"I will *not*. No—and I don't want—lie down jus' for few minutes. I'm goin' sit here till these—ah—foolish legs 'mine straighten 'emselves out—then 'm going home." ...

"Here's your beer, bo'," P. Sybarite's waiter announced.

"Keep the change," said the guest, tendering a quarter.

"T'anks"—with a look of surprise. Then familiarly knuckling the top of the table, the waiter stroked a rusty chin and surveyed the room. "There's Red, now," he observed.

"Where?"

"Over there with the skirt and the kid souse. Yuh kin see for yourself he's busy. D' yuh want I sh'u'd stir him up now?"

"Oh, yes," said P. Sybarite, in the tone of one recognising an oversight. "What's doing over there—anything?" he proceeded casually.

The waiter favoured him with a hard stare. "Red November's business ain't none'r mine," he growled; "an' less you know him a heluva sight better'n I do, you'd better take a straight tip from me and—*leave—it—lay*!"

"Oh!" said the little man hastily—"I was only wondering.... But I wish you would slip Red the high sign: all I want is one word with him."

"All right, bo'—you're on."

Slouching off, obviously reluctant to interrupt the diversions of Mr. November, the man at length mustered up courage to touch that gentleman's elbow. The gangster turned sharply, a frown replacing the smile which had illuminated his attempts to overcome the boy's recently developed aversion to drink. The waiter murmured in his private ear.

Promptly P. Sybarite received a sharp look from eyes as black and hard as shoe buttons; and with equanimity endured it— even went to the length of a nod accompanied by his quaint, ingratiating smile. A courtesy ignored completely: the dark eyes veered back to the waiter's face and the white teeth flashed as he was curtly dismissed.

He shuffled back, scowling, reported sulkily: "Says yuh gotta wait"; and turned away in answer to a summons from another table.

Unruffled, P. Sybarite sipped his beer—sipped it sparingly and not without misgivings, but sedulously to keep in character as a familiar of the dive.

Presently there came yet another lull in the clatter of tongues; and again the accents of the boy sounded distinctly from the gangster's table:

"I won't—that's flat! I refuse positively—go up stairs—sleep it off. I'm a' right—give you m' word—in the *head*. All my trouble's—these mutinous dogs of legs. But I'll make 'em mind, yet. Trust me—"

And again the babel blotted out his utterance.

But P. Sybarite had experienced a sudden rush of intelligence to the head—was in the throes of that mental process which it is our habit wittily to distinguish by the expressive term, "putting two and two together."

Could this, by any chance, be "that boy" who, Mr. Brian Shaynon had been assured, wouldn't know where he'd been when he waked? Was an attempt to ensure that desired consummation through the agency of a drug, being made in the open restaurant?

If not, why was Red November neglecting all other affairs to press drink upon a man who knew when he had enough?

If so, what might be the nature of the link connecting the boy with the "job," to be on which at half-past two November had just now covenanted with Brian Shaynon?

What incriminating knowledge could this boy possess, to render old Shaynon, willing that his memory should be expurgated by such a mind- and nerve-shattering agent as the knock-out drop of White Light commerce?

Now Shaynon was capable of almost any degree of infamy, if not, perhaps, the absolute peer of Red November.

This strange development of that night of Destiny began to assume in P. Sybarite's esteem a complexion of baleful promise.

But the more keenly interested he grew, the more indifferent he made himself appear, slouching low and lower in his chair, his eyes listless and half closed—his look one of the most pronounced apathy: the while he conned the circumstances, physical as well as psychical, with the narrowest attention. Certainly, it would seem, a man who had enough instinctive decency to wish to escape the degradation of deeper drunkenness, should be humoured rather than opposed....

The table on which his attention was focussed stood against the wall, the young man sitting in the corner between November and the woman. Of two tables between it and P. Sybarite's, one was vacant, the other occupied by a brace of hatchet-faced male intimates of the dive and creatures of November's—or their looks libelled them shamefully.

It seemed unlikely that the boy could get away against the wishes of the gang leader, however steadfastly he might stand upon his determination to drink no more. For nothing was to be hoped for from the sots, prostitutes, and parasites who made up the balance of that company: one and all, either too indifferent or too sophisticated, if not in active sympathy with the practices of the establishment, to lift a hand to interfere....

Testimony in support of this inference P. Sybarite received within the next few minutes, when the boy's temper abruptly veered from good-natured obduracy to open irritation.

"Damn it, no!" he cried in a high voice and with an impatient movement struck the glass from November's hand.

Though it went to the floor with a splintering crash, the incident attracted little more than casual glances from those at neighbouring tables....

November's countenance, however, turned grey with anger beneath its olive shade.

Momentarily his glance clashed with the woman's; and of a sudden the paint upon her cheeks and lips stood out as starkly artificial as carmine splashed upon a whitewashed wall. At the same time he flashed a like warning to his two followers at the next table; and the legs of their chairs grated on the tiled flooring as they shifted position, making ready for the signal to "mix in."

At this, P. Sybarite rose and nonchalantly moved over to November; his approach remarked by the latter with an evil leer; by the woman with a start of consternation; by the boy with sudden suspicion. Indubitably this last was beginning to question a hospitality that would not permit him to do as to him seemed best. With relief P. Sybarite noted symptoms of this dawning distrust. It made the problem simpler, to have the boy alive to his peril.

Pausing, P. Sybarite met November's glare with eyes informed with an expression amazingly remote and dispassionate, and in a level and toneless voice addressed him.

"I've a message for you—a hurry call—won't keep—"

"Well?" snapped the gangster. "What's it about? Spit it out!"

"Why, Nella says—" P. Sybarite began deliberately; and paused to cough politely behind his hand; and leaned confidentially over the table.

At this juncture the boy pushed back his chair and rose.

"Pardon me, m' dear," he said thickly to the woman; "'m goin' home."

"Ah, sit down," November interrupted quickly, pitching his protean accents to a key of cajolery—"sit down and have another. What's your hurry?"

His eyes caught the woman's.

"That's right, dearie," she chimed in hurriedly, laying a soft detaining hand on the boy's forearm. "Be a good fellow. Stake me to just one more pint—"

"No," the boy insisted, shaking free—"I'm going home. Le' me alone."

"Nella," P. Sybarite interpolated in an imperative tone, momentarily distracting November's attention—"Nella says to tell you she wants you—now—immediately. Do you get that?"

"Damn Nella!" snapped the gang leader. "Tell her to go to the devil. And you"—he menaced P. Sybarite with a formidable look—"you slide outa here—in a hurry! See?"

With this, rising in his place, he put forth a hand to detain the boy, who was sullenly pushing past the woman.

"Wait!" he insisted. "You can't go before you pay up—"

Whipping from his pocket a note (of what denomination he never knew—but it was large) P. Sybarite slapped it down upon the table.

"That'll pay whatever he owes," he announced, and to the boy: "Clear out—quick—do you hear!—while you've got a chance—"

"What t'ell business is it of yours?" November demanded, turning upon him furiously.

With an enigmatic smile, P. Sybarite dexterously tipped up his side of the table and, overturning it, caught the gangster unprepared for any such manoeuvre and pinned him squirming in the angle of wall and floor.

Immediately the woman came to her feet shrieking; while the little man seized the befuddled boy and swung him toward the door actually before he realised what was happening.

Simultaneously, November's henchmen at the adjoining table leapt into the brawl with an alacrity that sent their chairs clattering back upon the floor.

But in his magnificent assurance P. Sybarite had foreseen and planned cunningly against precisely that same contingency. No sooner had he sent the boy staggering on his way than he whirled completely round with a ready guard—and in no more than the very wink of exigence.

Already one of the creatures was almost on his back—the other hanging off and singularly employed (it seemed, considering) with his hands; just what he was up to P. Sybarite had time neither to see nor to surmise.

Sidestepping a wild swing, he planted a left full on the nose of the nearer assailant and knocked him backwards over a sprawling chair. Then turning attention to the other, he was barely in time to duck an uppercut—and out of the corners of his eyes caught the glint of brass-knuckles on the fist that failed to land.

Infuriated, he closed in, sent a staggering left to the thug's heart and a murdcrous right to his chin, so that he reeled and fell as if shot—while P. Sybarite with a bound again caught the boy by the arm and whirled him out through the doorway into the hall.

"Hurry!" he panted. "We've one chance in ten thousand—"

Beyond doubt they had barely that.

Hardened though they were to scenes of violence, the clients of the dive had stilled in apprehension the moment November lifted his voice in anger; while P. Sybarite's first overtly offensive move had struck them all dumb in terror.

Red November was one who had shot down his man in cold blood on the steps of the Criminal Courts Building and, through the favour of The Organisation that breeds such pests, escaped scot-free under the convenient fiction of "suspended sentence"; and knowing well the nature and the power of the man, the primal concerted thought had been to flee the place before bullets began to fly. In blind panic like that of sheep, they rose as one in uproar and surged toward the outer doors. November himself, struggling up from beneath the table, was caught and swept on willy-nilly in the front rank of the stampede. In a thought he found himself wedged tight in a press clogging the door. Before his enraged vision P. Sybarite was winning away with the boy.

Maddened, the gang leader managed to free his right arm and send a haphazard shot after them.

Only the instinctive recoil of those about him deflected his aim.

The report was one with a shock of shattered plate-glass: the soft-nosed bullet, splashing upon the glazed upper half of the door, caused the entire pane to collapse and disappear with the quickness of magic.

Halting, P. Sybarite wheeled and dropped a hand to the pocket wherein rested Mrs. Inche's automatic.

"Get that door open!" he cried to the boy. "I've got a taxi waiting—"

His words were drowned out by the thunderous detonations set up by a second shot in that constricted space.

With a thick sob, the boy reeled and swung against the wall as sharply as though he had been struck with a sledge-hammer.

Whimpering with rage, P. Sybarite tugged at the weapon; but it stuck fast, caught the lining of his coat-pocket.

Most happily before he could get it in evidence, the door was thrust sharply in, and through it with a rush materialised that most rare of metropolitan phenomena—the policeman on the spot.

Young and ardent, with courage as unique as his ubiquity, he blustered in like a whirlwind, brushing P. Sybarite to one side, the wounded boy to the other, and pausing only a single instant to throw back the skirts of his tunic and grasp the butt of the revolver in his hip-pocket, demanded in the voice of an Irish stentor:

"*What's-all-this? What's-all-this-now?*"

"Robbery!" P. Sybarite replied, mastering with difficulty a giggle of hysterical relief. "Robbery and attempted murder! Arrest that man—Red November—with the gun in his hand."

With an inarticulate roar, the patrolman swung on toward the gangster—and P. Sybarite plucked the boy by the sleeve and drew him quickly to the sidewalk.

By the never-to-be-forgotten grace of *Kismet* his taxicab was precisely where he had left it, the chauffeur on the seat.

"Quick!" he ordered the reeling boy—"into that cab unless you want to be treated by a Bellevue sawbones—held as a witness besides. Are you badly hurt?"

"Not badly," gasped the boy—"shot through the shoulder— can wait for treatment—must keep out of the papers—"

"Right!" P. Sybarite jerked open the door, and his charge stumbled into the cab. "Drive anywhere—like sin," he told the chauffeur—"tell you where to stop when we get clear of this mess—"

Privately he blessed that man; for the cab was in motion almost before he could swing clear of the sidewalk. He tumbled in upon the floor, and picked himself up in time to close the door only when they were swinging on two wheels round the corner of Seventh Avenue.

XV

SUCH STUFF AS PLOTS ARE MADE OF

"How is it?" P. Sybarite asked solicitously.

"Aches," replied the boy huddled in his corner of the cab.

Then he found spirit enough for a pale, thin smile, faintly visible in a milky splash from an electric arc rocking by the vehicle in its flight.

"Aches like hell," he added. "Makes one feel a bit sickish."

"Anything I can do?"

"No—thanks. I'll be all right—as soon as I find a surgeon to draw that slug and plaster me up."

"That's the point: where am I to take you?"

"Home—the Monastery—Forty-third Street."

"Bachelor apartments?"

"Yes; I herd by my lonesome."

"Praises be!" muttered P. Sybarite, relieved.

For several minutes he had been entertaining a vision of

himself escorting this battered and bloody young person to a home of shrieking feminine relations, and poignantly surmising the sort of welcome apt to be accorded the good Samaritan in such instances.

And while he was about it, he took time briefly to offer up thanks that the shock of his wound seemed to have sobered the boy completely.

Opening the door, he craned his neck out to establish communication with the ear of the chauffeur; to whom he repeated the address, adding an admonition to avoid the Monastery until certain he had shaken off pursuit, if any; and dodged back.

At this juncture the taxicab was slipping busily up Eighth Avenue, having gained that thoroughfare via Forty-first Street. A little later it turned eastwards....

"No better, I presume?" P. Sybarite enquired.

"Not so's you'd notice it," the boy returned bravely.... "First time anything like this ever happened to me," he went on. "Funny sensation—precisely as if somebody had lammed me for a home run—with a steel girder for a bat ..."

"Must be tough!" said P. Sybarite blankly, experiencing a qualm at the thought of a soft-nosed bullet mushrooming through living flesh.

"Guess I can stand it.... Where are we?"

P. Sybarite took observations."

"Forty-seventh, near Sixth Avenue," he reported finally.

"Good: we'll be home in five minutes."

"Think you can hold out that long?"

"Sure—got to; if I keel over before we reach my digs ... chances are it'll get you into trouble ... besides, I want to fight shy of the papers ... no good airing this scandal ..."

"None whatever," affirmed P. Sybarite heartily. "But—how did you get into it?"

"Just by way of being a natural-born ass."

"Oh, well! If it comes to that, I admit it's none of my business—"

"The deuce it isn't! After all you've done for me! Good Lord, man, where *would* I be...!"

"Sleeping the sleep of the doped in some filthy corner of Dutch House, most likely."

"And you saved me from that!"

"And got this hole drilled through you instead."

"Got me away; I'd've collected the lead anyhow—wasn't meaning to stay without a fight."

"Then you weren't as drunk as you seemed?"

"Didn't you catch me making a move the minute you created a diversion? Of course, I'd no idea you were friendly—"

"Look here," P. Sybarite interrupted sharply: "doesn't it hurt you to talk?"

"No—helps me forget this ache."

"All right, then—tell me how this came about. What has Red November got on you, to make him so anxious—?"

"Nothing, as far as I know; unless it was Brian Shaynon's doing—"

"A-ah!"

"You know that old blighter?"

"Slightly—very slightly."

"Friend of yours?"

"Not exactly."

The accent of P. Sybarite's laugh rendered the disclaimer conclusive.

"Glad to hear that," said the boy gravely: "I'd despise to be beholden to any friend of his ..."

"Well.... But what's the trouble between you and old man Shaynon?"

"Search me—unless he thought I was spying on him. I say!" the boy exclaimed excitedly—"what business could he have had with Red November there, to-night?"

"That *is* a question," P. Sybarite allowed.

"Something urgent, I'll be bound!—else he wouldn't ever have dared show his bare map in that dump."

"One would think so...."

"I'd like to figure this thing out. Perhaps you can help. To begin with—I went to a party to-night."

"I know," said P. Sybarite, with a quiet chuckle: "the Hadley-Owen masquerade."

"How did you know?"

"*Kismet!* It had to be."

"Are you by any chance—mad?"

"I shouldn't be surprised. Anyhow, I'm a bit mad I wasn't invited. Everybody I know or meet—almost—is either bidden to that party or knows somebody who is. Forgive the interruption.... Anyway," he added, "we're here."

The taxicab was drawing up before an apartment house entrance.

Hastily recovering his hoard of gold-pieces, P. Sybarite jumped out and presented one to the driver.

"Can't change that," said the latter, staring. "Besides, this was a charge call."

"I know," said P. Sybarite apologetically; "but this is for you."

"Good God!" cried the chauffeur.

"And yet," mused P. Sybarite, "they'd have you believe all taxicab chauffeurs mercenary!"

Recklessly he forced the money into the man's not altogether inhospitable palm.

"For being a good little tight-mouth," he explained gravely.

"Forever and ever, amen!" protested the latter fervently. "And thank *you*!"

"If you're satisfied, we're quits," returned P. Sybarite, offering a hand to the boy.

"I can manage," protested this last, descending without

assistance. "And it's better so," he explained as they crossed to the door; "I don't want the hallboys here to suspect—and I can hold up a few minutes longer, never fear."

"Business of taking off my hat to you," said P. Sybarite in unfeigned admiration; "for pure grit, you're a young wonder."

A liveried hallboy opened the door. A second waited in the elevator. Promptly ascending, they were set down at one of the upper floors.

Throughout the boy carried himself with never a quiver, his countenance composed and betraying what pain he suffered only to eyes keen to discern its trace of pallor. Now as he left the elevator and fitted a key to the lock of his private front door, he addressed the attendant, over his shoulder, in a manner admirably casual:

"By the way, Jimmy—"

"Sir?"

"Call up Dr. Higgins for me."

"Yes, sir."

"Tell him I've an attack of indigestion and will be glad if he'll turn out and see if he can't fix me up for the night."

"Very good, Mr. Kenny."

The gate clanged and the cage dropped from sight as Mr. Kenny opened the door and stood aside to let P. Sybarite precede him.

"Rot!" objected the little man forcibly. "Go in and turn up the lights. Punctilio from a man in your condition—!"

The boy nodded wearily, passed in, and switched up the lights in a comfortably furnished sitting-room.

"As a matter of fact," he said thoughtfully, when P. Sybarite had followed him in and shut the door—"I'm wondering how much of a bluff I may be, after all."

"Meaning—?"

"By all literary precedent I ought to faint now, after my magnificent exhibition of superhuman endurance. But I'm not going to."

"That's rather sporting of you," P. Sybarite grinned.

"Not at all; I just don't want to—don't feel like it. That sick feeling is gone—nothing but a steady agony like a hot iron through my shoulder—something any man with teeth to grit could stand."

"We'll find out soon enough. I don't pretend to be any sort of a dab at repairs on punctured humanity, but I read enough popular fiction myself to know that the only proper thing to do is to ruin that handsome coat of yours by cutting it off your back. We can anticipate the doctor to that extent, at least."

"That's one thing, at least, that the popular novelist knows *right*," asserted Mr. Kenny with conviction. "Sorry for the coat—but you'll find scissors yonder, on my desk."

And when P. Sybarite fetched them, he sat himself sideways in a straight-backed chair and cheerfully endured the little man's impromptu essays in first-aid measures.

A very little snipping and slashing sufficed to do away with the shoulder and sleeve of the boy's coat and to lay open his waistcoat as well, exposing a bloodstained shirt. And then, at the instant when P. Sybarite was noting with relief that the stain showed both in back and in front, the telephone shrilled.

"If you don't mind answering that—" grunted Mr. Kenny.

P. Sybarite was already at the instrument.

"Yes?" he answered. "Dr. Higgins?"

"Sorry, sir," replied a strange voice: "Dr. Higgins isn't in yet. Any message?"

"Tell him Mr. Kenny needs him at the Monastery, and the matter's urgent.... Doctor not in," he reported superfluously, returning to cut away collar, tie, shirt, and undershirt. "Never mind, I shouldn't be surprised if we could manage to do without him, after all."

"Meaning it's not so bad—?"

"Meaning," said the other, exposing the naked shoulder, "I'm beginning to hope you've had a marvellously narrow escape."

"Feels like it," said Kenny, ironic.

P. Sybarite withheld response while he made close examination. At the base of Mr. Kenny's neck, well above the shoulder-blade, dark blood was welling slowly from an ugly puncture. And in front there was a corresponding puncture, but smaller. And presently his deft and gentle fingers, exploring the folds of the boy's undershirt, closed upon the bullet itself.

"I don't believe," he announced, displaying his find, "you deserve such luck. Somehow you managed to catch this just right for it to slip through without either breaking bone or severing artery. And by a special dispensation of an all-wise Providence, Red November must have been preoccupied when he loaded that gun, for somehow a steel-jacketed instead of a soft-nosed bullet got into the chamber he wasted on you. Otherwise you'd have been pretty badly smashed. As it is, you'll probably be laid up only a few days."

"I told you I wasn't so badly hurt—"

"God's good to the Irish. Where's your bathroom?"

With a gesture Kenny indicated its location.

"And handkerchiefs—?"

"Upper bureau drawer in the bedroom."

In a twinkling P. Sybarite was off and back again with materials for an antiseptic wash and a rude bandage.

"How'd you know I was Irish?" demanded the patient.

"By yoursilf's name," quoth P. Sybarite in a thick brogue as natural as grass, while he worked away busily. "'Tis black Irish, and well I know it. 'Twas me mither's maiden name—Kenny. She had a brother, Michael he was and be way av bein' a rich conthractor in this very town as ever was, befure he died— God rist his sowl! He left two children—a young leddy who mis-spells her name M-a-e A-l-y-s—keep still!—and Peter, yersilf, me cousin, if it's not mistaken I am."

"The Lord save us!" said the boy. "You're never Percy Sybarite!"

P. Sybarite winced. "Not so loud!" he pleaded in a stage whisper. "Some one might hear you."

"What the devil's the matter with you?"

"I am that man you named—but, prithee, Percy me no Percevals, an' you'd be my friend. For fifteen years I've kept my hideous secret well. If it becomes public now ..."

Peter Kenny laughed in spite of his pain.

"I'll keep your secret, too," he volunteered, "since you feel that way about it.... But, I say: what have you been doing with yourself since—since—" He stammered.

"Since the fall of the House of Sybarite?"

"Yes. I didn't know you were in New York, even."

"Your mother and Mae Alys knew it—but kept it quiet, the same as me," said the little man.

"But—well—what *have* you been doing, then?"

"Going to and fro like a raging lion—more or less—seeking what I might devour."

"And the devourings have been good, eh? You're high-spirited enough."

"I think," said P. Sybarite quietly—"I may say—though you can't see it—that my present smile would, to a shrewd observer, seem to indicate I'd swallowed a canary-bird ... a nice, fat, golden canary-bird!" he repeated, smacking his lips with unction.

"You talk as if you'd swallowed a dictagraph," said Peter Kenny.

"It's my feeling," sighed P. Sybarite. "But yourself? Let's see; when I saw you last you were the only authentic child pest of your day and generation—six or seven at most. How long have you been out of college?"

"A year—not quite."

"And sporting bachelor rooms of your own!"

"I'm of age. Besides, if you must know, mother and Mae Alys are both dotty on the society game, and I'm not. I won't be rushed round to pink teas and—and all that sort of thing."

"Far more wholesome than pink whiskeys at Dutch House."

"You don't understand—"

"No; but I mean to. There!" announced P. Sybarite, finishing the bandage with a tidy flat knot—make yourself comfortable on that couch, tell me where you keep your whiskey, and I'll mix myself a drink and listen to your degrading confession....

"Now," he added, when Peter Kenny, stretched out on the couch, had suffered himself to be covered up—"not being an M.D., I've no conscience at all about letting you talk yourself to death; eaten alive as I am with curiosity; and knowing besides that you can't kill a Kenny but with kindness."

"You'll find the whiskey on the buffet," said the boy.

"Obliged to you," P. Sybarite replied, finding it.

"And I suppose I—"

"You're quite right; you've had enough. Alcohol is nothing to help mend a wound. If your friend Higgins permits it, when he comes—well and good.... Meanwhile," he added, taking a seat near the head of the couch, and fixing his youthful relation with a stern enquiringeye—"what were you doing in Dutch House the night?"

"I've been trying to tell you—"

"And now you must.... Is there a cigar handy?... Thanks.... This whiskey is prime stuff.... Go on. I'm waiting."

"Well," Peter Kenny confessed sheepishly. "I'm in love—"

"And you proposed to her to-night at the ball?"

"Yes, and—"

"She refused you."

"Yes, but—"

"So you decided to do the manly thing—go out and pollute yourself with drink?"

"That's about the size of it," Peter admitted, shamefaced.

"It's no good reason," announced P. Sybarite. "Now, if you'd been celebrating your happy escape, I'd be the last to blame you."

"You don't understand, and you won't give me a chance—"

"I'm waiting—all ears—but not the way *you* mean."

"It wasn't as if she'd left me any excuse to hope ... but she told me flat she didn't care for me."

"That's bad, Peter. Forgive my ill-timed levity: I didn't mean it meanly, boy," P. Sybarite protested.

"It's worse than you think," Peter complained. "I can stand her not caring for me. Why should she?"

"Why, indeed?"

"It's because she's gone and promised to marry Bayard Shaynon."

P. Sybarite looked dazed.

"She? Bayard Shaynon? Who's the girl?"

"Marian Blessington. Why do you ask? Do you know her?"

There was a pause. P. Sybarite blinked furiously.

"I've heard that name," he said quietly, at length. "Isn't she old Brian's ward—the girl who disappeared recently?"

"She didn't disappear, really. She's been staying with friends—told me so herself. That's all the foundation the *Journal* had for its story."

"Friends?"

"So she said."

"Did she name them?"

"No—"

"Or say where?"

"No; but some place out of town, of course."

"Of course," P. Sybarite repeated mechanically. He eyed fixedly the ash on the end of his cigar. "And she told you she meant to marry Bayard Shaynon, did she!"

"She said she'd promised.... And that," the boy broke out, "was what drove me crazy. He's—he's—well, you know what he is."

"His father's son," said P. Sybarite gloomily.

"He was there to-night—the old man, too; and after what Marian had told me, I just couldn't trust myself to meet or speak to either of them. So I bolted back here, took a stiff drink, changed from costume to these clothes, and went out to make a besotted ass of myself. Naturally I landed in Dutch House. And there—the first thing I noticed when I went in was old Shaynon, sitting at the same table you took, later—waiting. Imagine my surprise—I'd left him at the Bizarre not thirty minutes before!"

"I'm imagining it, Peter. Get ahead."

"I hailed him, but he wouldn't recognise me—simply glared. Presently Red November came in and they went upstairs together. So I stuck around, hoping to get hold of Red and make him drunk enough to talk. Curiously enough when Shaynon left, Red came directly to my table and sat down. But by that time I'd had some champagne on top of whiskey and was beginning to know that if I pumped in anything more, it'd be November's party instead of mine. And when he tried to insist on my drinking more, I got scared—feeling what I'd had as much as I did."

"You're not the fool you try to seem," P. Sybarite conceded. "I heard November promise Shaynon, at the door, that you wouldn't remember much when you came to. The old scoundrel didn't want to be seen—hadn't expected to be recognised and, when he found you'd followed, planned to fix things so that you'd never tell on him."

"But *why*?"

"That's what I'm trying to figure out. There's some sort of shenanigan brewing, or my first name's Peter, the same as yours—which I wish it was so.... Be quiet a bit and let me think."

For a little while P. Sybarite sat pondering with vacant eyes; and the wounded boy stared upward with a frown, as though endeavouring to puzzle the answer to this riddle out of the blankness of the ceiling.

"What time does this Hadley-Owen party break up?"

"Not till daylight. It's the last big fixture of the social season, and ordinarily they keep it up till sunrise."

"It'll be still going, then?"

"Strong. They'll be in full swing, now, of after-supper dancing."

"That settles it: I'm going."

The boy lifted on his elbow in amaze, then subsided with a grunt of pain.

"*You're* going?"

"You say you've got a costume of some sort here? I'll borrow it. We're much of a size."

"Heaven knows you're welcome, but—"

"But what?"

"You have no invitation."

Rising, P. Sybarite smiled loftily. "Don't worry about that. If I can't bribe my way past a cordon mercenary foreign waiters—and talk down any other opposition—I'm neither as flush as I think nor as Irish."

"But what under the sun do you want there?"

"To see what's doing—find out for myself what devilment Brian Shaynon's hatching. Maybe I'll do no good—and maybe I'll be able to put a spoke in his wheel. To do that—once— *right*—I'd be willing to die as poor as I've lived till this blessed night!"

He paused an instant on the threshold of his cousin's bedroom; turned back a sombre visage.

"I've little love for Brian Shaynon, myself, or none. You know what he did to me—and mine."

XVI

BEELZEBUB

Late enough in all conscience was the last guest to arrive for the Hadley-Owen masquerade.

Already town-cars, carriages, and private 'busses were being called for and departing with their share of the more seasoned and sober-sided revellers, to whom bed and appetite for breakfast had come to mean more than a chance to romp through a cotillion by the light of the rising sun—to say discreetly little or nothing of those other conveyances which had borne away *their* due proportion of far less sage and by no means sober-sided ones, who yet retained sufficient sense of the fitness of things to realise that bed followed by matutinal bromides would be better for them than further dalliance with the effervescent and evanescent spirits of festivity.

More and more frequently the elevators, empty but for their attendants, were flying up to the famous ball-room floor of the Bizarre, to descend heavy-laden with languid laughing parties of gaily-costumed ladies and gentlemen no less brilliantly attired—prince and pauper, empress and shepherdess, monk, milkmaid, and mountebank: all weary yet reluctant in their going.

And at this hour a smallish gentleman, in an old-style Inverness opera-coat that cloaked him to his ankles, with an opera hat set jauntily a wee bit askew on his head, a mask of crimson silk covering his face from brows to lips, slipped silently like some sly, sinister shadow through the Fifth Avenue portals of the Bizarre, and shaped a course by his wits across the lobby to the elevators, so discreetly and unobtrusively that none of the flunkeys in attendance noticed his arrival.

In effect, he didn't arrive at all, but suddenly was there.

A car, discharging its passengers before the smallish gentleman could catch the eye of its operator, flew suddenly upward in the echo of a gate slammed shut in his face; and all the other cars were still at the top, according to the bronze arrows of their tell-tale dials. The late arrival held up patiently; but after an instant's deliberation, doffed his hat, crushed it flat, slipped out of his voluminous cloak, and beckoned a liveried attendant.

In the costume thus disclosed, he cut an impish figure: "Satan on the half-shell," Peter Kenny had christened him.

A dress coat of black satin fitted P. Sybarite more neatly than him for whom it had been made. The frilled bosom of his shirt was set with winking rubies, and the lace cuffs at his wrists were caught together with rubies—whether real or false, like coals of fire: and ruby was the hue both of his satin mask and his satin small-clothes. Buckles of red paste brilliants burned on the insteps of his slender polished shoes with scarlet heels; and his snug black silk stockings set off ankles and calves so well-turned that the Prince of Sin himself might have taken pride in them. For boutonniere he wore a smouldering ember—so true an imitation that at first he himself had hesitated to touch it. Literally to crown all, his ruddy hair was twisted upward from each temple in a cornuted fashion that was most vividly picturesque.

"Here," he said, surrendering hat and coat to the servitor before the latter could remonstrate—"take and check these for me, please. I shan't be going for some time yet."

"Sorry, sir, but the cloak-room down 'ere's closed, sir. You'll have to check them on the ball-room floor above."

"No matter," said the little man: and groping in a pocket, he produced a dollar bill and tendered it to ready fingers; "you keep 'em for me, down here. It'll save time when I'm ready to go."

"Very good, sir. Thank you."

"You won't forget me?"

The flunkey grinned. "You're the only gentleman I've seen to-night, sir, in a costume anything like your own."

"There's but one of me in the Union," said the gentleman, sententious: "my spear knows no brother."

"Thank you, sir," said the servant civilly, making off.

With an air of some dubiety, the little man watched him go.

"I say!" he cried suddenly—"come back!"

He was obeyed.

A second dollar bill appeared as it were by magic between his fingers. The flunkey stared.

"Beg pardon, sir?"

"Take it"—impatiently.

"Thank you." The well-trained fingers executed their most familiar manoeuvre. "But—m'y I ask, sir—wot's it for?"

"You called me a gentleman just now."

"Yes, sir."

"You were right."

"Quite so, sir."

"The devil *is* a gentleman," the masquerader insisted firmly.

"So I've always 'eard, sir."

"Then you may go; you've earned the other dollar."

Obsequiousness stared: "M'y I ask, 'ow so?"

"By standing for that antediluvian bromidiom. I had to get it off my chest to somebody, or else blow up. Far better to hire an audience when you can't be original. Remember that; you've been paid: you daren't object."

"Thankyousir," said the lackey blankly.

"And now—avaunt—before I brand thee for mine own!"

The little gentleman flung out an imperative, melodramatic arm; and veritable sparks sprayed from his crackling finger-tips. The servant retired in haste and dismay.

"E's balmy—or screwed—or the Devil 'imself!" he muttered....

Beneath his mask the little man grinned privately at the man's retreat.

"Piker!" said he severely—"sharpening your wits on helpless servants. A waiter has no friends, anyway!"

An elevator, descending, discharged into the lobby half a dozen mirthful maskers. Of these, a Scheherazade of bewitching prettiness (in a cloak of ermine!) singled out the silent, cynical little gentleman in scarlet mask and smalls, and menaced him merrily with a jewelled forefinger.

"What—you, Lucifer! Traitor! Where have you been all evening?"

"Madame!"—he bowed mockingly—"in spirit, always at your ear."

She flushed and bit her lip in charming confusion; while an abbess, with face serene in the frame of her snowy coif, caught up the ball of badinage:

"Ah, in spirit! But in the flesh?"

"Why, poppet!" he retorted in suave surprise—"it isn't possible that *you* missed me?"

And she, too, coloured; while a third, a girl dressed all in buckskin from beaded hunting-shirt to fringed leggings and dainty moccasins, bent to peer into his face.

"Who are you?" she demanded curiously. "I don't seem to know you—"

"That, child, you have already proved."

"I?... Proved?... How do you mean?"

"You alone have not yet blushed."

And wheeling mischievously to the others, he covered them with widespread hands in burlesque benediction.

"The unction of my deep damnation abide with ye, my children, now and forevermore!" he chanted, showering sparks from crepitant finger-tips; and bounded lightly into the elevator.

"But your mask!" protested Scheherazade in a pet. "You've no right—when we all unmasked at supper."

Through the iron fretwork of the gate, the little gentleman shot a Parthian spark or two.

"I wear no mask!" he informed them solemnly as the car shot from sight.

The conceit tickled him; he had it still in mind when he alighted at the ball-room floor.

Pausing in the anteroom, he struck an artificial pose on his high red heels and stroked thin, satiric lips with slender fingers, reviewing the crush with eyes that glinted light-hearted malice through the scarlet visor; seeking a certain one and finding her not among those many about him—their gay exotic trappings half hidden beneath wraps of modern convention assumed against impending departure.

A hedge of backs hid from him the ball-room, choking the wide, high arch of its entrance.

Turning to one side, he began to pick a slow way through the press, and so presently found himself shoulder to shoulder with elderly and pompous Respectability in a furred great-coat; who, all ready for the street, with shining topper poised at breast-level, had delayed his going for an instant's guarded confabulation with a youngish man conspicuous in this, that he, alone of all that company, was in simple evening dress.

Their backs were toward P. Sybarite, but by the fat pink folds above the back of Respectability's collar and the fat white side-whiskers adorning his plump pink chops, Beelzebub knew that he encountered for the second time that evening Respectability of the gold-capped cane.

Without the least shame, he paused and cocked sharp ears to catch what he could of the conversation between these two.

Little enough he profited by his open eavesdropping; what he heard was scarcely illuminating when applied to the puzzle that haunted him.

"She won't—that's flat," Respectability's companion announced in a sullen voice.

By the tone of this last Beelzebub knew that it issued from an ugly twisted mouth.

"But," Respectability insisted heavily—"You're sure you've done your best to persuade her?"

"She won't listen to reason."

"Well ... everything's arranged. You have me to thank for that."

"Oh," sneered the younger man, "you've done a lot, you have!"

And then, moving to give way to another making toward the elevators, Brian Shaynon discovered at his elbow that small attentive body in sinister scarlet and black.

For a breath, utterance failed the old man. He glared pop-eyed indignation from a congested countenance, his fat lips quivering and his jowls as well; and then as Beelzebub tapped him familiarly if lightly upon the chest, his face turned wholly purple, from swollen temples to pendulous chin.

"Well met, *ame damnee*!" P. Sybarite saluted him gaily. "Are you indeed off so early upon my business?"

"Damnation!" exclaimed Brian Shaynon, all but choking.

"It shall surely be your portion," gravely assented the little man. "To all who in my service prosper in a worldly way— damnation, upon my honourable Satanic word!"

"Who the devil—?"

"*Whisht!*" P. Sybarite reproved. "A trifle more respect, if you please—lest you wake in the morning to find all my benefactions turned to ashes in your strong-boxes!"

But here Respectability found his full voice.

"Who are you?" he demanded so stormily that heads turned curiously his way. "I demand to know! Remove that mask! Impertinent—!"

"Mask?" purred Beelzebub in a tone of wonder. "I wear no mask!"

"No mask!" stammered the older man, in confusion.

"Nay, *I* am frankly what I am—old Evil's self," P. Sybarite explained blandly; "but you, Brian Shaynon—now you go always masked: waking or sleeping, hypocrisy's your lifelong mask. You see the distinction, old servant?"

In another moment he might have suffered a sound drubbing with the ebony cane but for Peter Kenny's parlour-magic trick. For as Brian Shaynon started forward to seize Beelzebub by the collar, a stream of incandescent sparks shot point-blank into his face; and when he fell back in puffing dismay, Beelzebub laughed provokingly, ducked behind the backs of a brace of highly diverted bystanders, and quickly and deftly wormed his way through the press to the dancing-floor itself.

As for the younger man—he of the unhandsome mouth—P. Sybarite was content to hold him in reserve, to be dealt with later, at his leisure. For the present, his business pressed with the waning night.

In high feather, bubbling with mischief, he sidled along the wall a little way, then halted to familiarise himself with scene and atmosphere against his next move.

But after the first minute or two, spent in silent review of the brilliant scene, his thin lips lost something of their cynic modelling, the eyes behind the scarlet visor something of their mischievous twinkle—softening with shadows envious and regretful.

The room was as one vast pool of limpid golden light, walls and ceilings so luminous with the refulgence of a thousand electric bulbs that they seemed translucent, glowing with a radiance from beyond.

On the famous floor, twelve-score couples swung and swayed to the intoxicating rhythms of an unseen orchestra; kaleido-scopic in their amazingly variegated costuming of colour, drifting past the lonely, diabolical little figure, an endless chain of paired anachronisms.

Searching narrowly each fair face that flashed past in another's arms, he waited with seeming patience. But the music buzzed in his brain and his toes tingled for it; breathing the warm, voluptuous air, he inhaled hints of a thousand agreeable and exciting scenes; watching, he perceived in perturbation the witchery of a hundred exquisite women. And a rancorous discontent gnawed at his famished heart.

This was all his by right of birth—should be his now, but for the blind malice of his sorry destiny. *Kismet* had favoured him greatly, but too late....

But of a sudden he forgot self-pity and vain repining, in the discovery of the one particular woman swinging dizzily past in the arms of an Incroyable, whose giddy plumage served only to render the more striking her exquisite fairness and the fine simplicity of her costume.

For she was all in the black-and-white uniform of a Blessington shopgirl; black skirt and blouse, stockings and pumps, relieved by showy linen at throat and wrists, with at waist the white patch of a tiny lace-and-linen apron.

Perhaps it was his start of recognition; it may have been the very fixed intensity of his regard; whatever drew it, her gaze veered to his silent and aloof figure, and for an instant his eyes held hers. At once, to his consternation, the hot blood stained her lovely face from throat to brow; her glance wavered, fell in confusion, then as though by a strong effort of will alone, steadied once more to his. Nodding with an air of friendly diffidence, she flashed him a strange, perplexing smile; and was swept on and away.

For a thought he checked his breath in stupefaction. Had she, then, recognised him? Was it possible that her intuition had been keen enough to pierce his disguise, vizard and all?

But the next moment he could have sworn in chagrined appreciation of his colossal stupidity. Of course!—his costume was that worn by Peter Kenny earlier in the evening; and as between Peter and himself, of the same stock, the two were much of a muchness in physique; both, moreover, were red-headed; their points of unlikeness were negligible, given a mask.

So after all, her emotion had been due solely to embarrassment and regret for the pain she had caused poor Peter by refusing his offer of marriage!

Well!... P. Sybarite drew a long, sane breath, laughed wholesomely at himself, and thereafter had eyes only to keep the girl in sight, however far and involved her wanderings through the labyrinth of the dance.

In good time the music ended; the fluent movement of the dancers subsided with a curious effect of eddying—like confetti settling to rest; and P. Sybarite left his station by the wall, slipping like quicksilver through the heart of the throng to the far side of the room, where, near a great high window wide to the night, the breathless shopgirl had dropped into a chair.

At Beelzebub's approach the Incroyable, perhaps mindful of obligations in another quarter, bowed and moved off, leaving the field temporarily quite clear.

She greeted him with a faint recurrence of her former blush.

"Why, Peter!" she cried—and so sealed with confirmation his surmise as to her mistake—"I was wondering what had become of you. I thought you must have gone home."

"Peter did go home," P. Sybarite affirmed gravely, bending over her hand.

His voice perplexed her tremendously. She opened eyes wide.

"Peter!" she exclaimed reproachfully—"you promised it wouldn't make any difference. We were to go on just as always—good friends. And now ..."

"Yes?" P. Sybarite prompted as she faltered.

"I don't like to say it, Peter, but—your voice is so different. You've not been—doing anything foolish, have you?"

"Peter hasn't," the little man lied cheerfully; "Peter went home to sulk like the unwhipped cub he is; and sulking, was yet decent enough to lend me these rags."

"You—you're not Peter Kenny?"

"No more than you are Molly Lessing."

"Molly Lessing! What do you know—? Who can you be? Why are you masked?"

"Simply," he explained pleasantly, "that my incognito may remain such to all save you."

"But—but who *are* you?"

"It is permitted?" he asked, with a gesture offering to take the tiny printed card of dance engagements that dangled from her fingers by its silken thong.

In dumb mystification the girl surrendered it.

Seating himself beside her, P. Sybarite ran his eye down the list.

"The last was number—which?" he enquired with unruffled impudence.

Half angry, half amused, wholly confused, she told him: "Fifteen."

"Then one number only remains."

His lips hardened as he read the initials pencilled opposite that numeral; they were "B.S."

"Bayard Shaynon?" he queried.

She assented with a nod, her brows gathering.

Coolly, with the miniature pencil attached to the card, he changed the small, faint *B* to a large black *P*, strengthened the *S* to correspond, and added to that *ybarite*; then with a bow returned the card.

The girl received the evidence of her senses with a silent gasp.

He bowed again: "Yours to command."

"You—Mr. Sybarite!"

"I, Miss Blessington."

"But—incredible!" she cried. "I can't believe you ..."

Facing her, he lifted his scarlet visor, meeting her stare with his wistful and diffident smile.

"You see," he said, readjusting the mask.

"But—what does this mean?"

"Do you remember our talk on the way home after *Kismet*—four hours or several years ago: which is it?"

"I remember we talked ..."

"And I—clumsily enough, Heaven knows!—told you that I'd go far for one who'd been kind and tolerant to me, if she were in trouble and could use my poor services?"

"I remember—yes."

"You suspected—surely—it was yourself I had in mind?"

"Why, yes; but—"

"And you'll certainly allow that what happened later, at the door, when I stood in the way of the importunate Mr. 'B.S.'—if I'm not sadly in error—was enough to convince any one that you needed a friend's good offices?"

"So," she said softly, with glimmering eyes—"so for that you followed me here, Mr. Sybarite!"

"I wish I might claim it. But it wouldn't be true. No—I didn't follow you."

"Please," she begged, "don't mystify me—"

"I don't mean to. But to tell the truth, my own head is still awhirl with all the chapter of accidents that brought me here. Since you flew off with B.S., following afoot, I've traversed a vast deal of adventure—to wind up here. If," he added, grinning, "this is the wind-up. I've a creepy, crawly feeling that it isn't...."

"Miss Blessington," he pursued seriously, "if you have patience to listen to what I've been through since we parted in Thirty-eighth Street—?" Encouraged by her silence he went on: "I've broken the bank at a gambling house; been held up for my winnings at the pistol's point—but managed to keep them. I've been in a raid and escaped only after committing felonious assault on two detectives. I then burglarised a private residence, and saved the mistress of the house from being murdered by her rascally husband—blundered thence to the deadliest dive in New York—met and slanged mine ancient enemy, the despoiler of my house—took part in a drunken brawl—saved my infatuated young idiot of a cousin, Peter Kenny, from assassination—took him home, borrowed his clothing, and impudently invited myself to this party on the mere suspicion that 'Molly Lessing' and Marian Blessington might be one and the same, after all!... And all, it appears, that I might come at last to beg a favour of you."

"I can't think what it can be," breathed the girl, dumfounded.

"To forgive my unpardonable impertinence—"

"I've not been conscious of it."

"You'll recognise it immediately. I am about to transgress your privacy with a question—two, in fact. Will you tell me, please, in confidence, why you refused my cousin, Peter Kenny, when he asked you to marry him?"

Colouring, she met his eyes honestly.

"Because—why, it was so utterly absurd! He's only a boy. Besides, I don't care for him—that way."

"You care for some one else—'that way'?"

"Yes," said the girl softly, averting her face.

"Is it—Mr. Bayard Shaynon?"

"No," she replied after a perceptible pause.

"But you have promised to marry him?"

"I once made him that promise—yes."

"You mean to keep it?"

"I must."

"Why?"

"It was my father's wish."

"And yet—you don't like him!"

Looking steadily before her, the girl said tensely: "I loathe him."

"Then," cried P. Sybarite in a joyful voice, "I may tell you something: you needn't marry him."

She turned startled eyes to his, incredulous.

"*Need* not?"

"I should have said *can* not—"

Through the loud hum of voices that, filling the room, had furnished a cover for their conversation, sounded the opening bars of music for the final dance.

The girl rose suddenly, eyes like stars aflame in a face of snow.

"He will be coming for me now," she said hurriedly. "But—if

you mean what you say—I must know—instantly—why you say it. How can we manage to avoid him?"

"This way," said P. Sybarite, indicating the wide window nearby.

Through its draped opening a shallow balcony showed, half-screened by palms whose softly stirring fronds, touched with artificial light, shone a garish green against the sombre sky of night.

Immediately Marian Blessington slipped through the hangings and, turning, beckoned P. Sybarite to follow.

"There's no one here," she announced in accents tremulous with excitement, when he joined her. "Now—*now* tell me what you mean!"

"One moment," he warned her gently, turning back to the window just as it was darkened by another figure.

The man with the twisted mouth stood there, peering blindly into the semi-obscurity.

"Marian...?" he called in a voice meant to be ingratiating.

"Well?" the girl demanded harshly.

"I thought I saw you," he commented blandly, advancing a pace and so coming face to face with the bristling little Mephistophelean figure, which he had endeavoured to ignore.

"My dance, I believe," he added a trace more brusquely, over the little man's head.

"I must ask you to excuse me," said the girl coldly.

"You don't care to dance again to-night?"

"Thank you—no."

"Then I will give myself the pleasure of sitting it out with you."

"I'm afraid you'll have to excuse me, Bayard," she returned, consistently inflexible.

He hesitated. "Do I understand you're ready for me to take you home?"

"You're to understand that I will neither dance nor sit out the dance with you—and that I don't wish to be disturbed."

"Bless your heart!" P. Sybarite interjected privately.

The voice of the younger Shaynon broke with passion.

"This is—the limit!" he cried violently. "I've reached the end of my endurance. Who's this creature you're with?"

"Is your memory so short?" P. Sybarite asked quietly. "Have you forgotten the microbe?—the little guy who puts the point in disappointment?"

"I've forgotten nothing, you—animal! Nor that you insulted my father publicly only a few minutes ago, you—"

"That is something that takes a bit of doing, too!" affirmed P. Sybarite with a nod.

"And I want to inform you, sir," Shaynon raged, "that you've gone too far by much. I insist that you remove your mask and tell me your name."

"And if I refuse?" said the little man coolly.

"If you refuse—or if you persist in this insolent attitude, sir!— I—I'll—"

"*What?* In the name of brevity, make up your mind and give it a name, man!"

"I'll thrash you within an inch of your life—here and now!" Shaynon blustered.

"One moment," P. Sybarite pleaded with a graceful gesture. "Before committing yourself to this mad enterprise, would you mind telling me exactly how you spell that word *inch*? With a capital *I* and a final *e*—by any chance?"

XVII

IN A BALCONY

Bewilderment and consternation, working in the man, first struck him dumb, aghast, and witless, then found expression in an involuntary gasp that was more than half of wondering fear, the remainder rage slipping its leash entirely:

"*What?*"

He advanced a pace with threatening mien.

Overshadowed though he was, P. Sybarite stood his ground with no least hint of dismay. To the contrary, he was seen to stroke his lips discreetly as if to erase a smile.

"The word in question," he said with exasperating suavity, "is the common one of four letters, to-wit, *inch*; as ordinarily spelled denoting the unit of lineal measurement—the twelfth part of a foot; but lend it a capital *I* and an ultimate *e*—my good fellow!—and it stands, I fear too patiently, for the standard of your blackguardism."

Speechless, the younger Shaynon hesitated, lifting an uncertain hand to his throat, as if to relieve a sense of strangulation.

"Or what if I were to suggest—delicately—that you're within an Inche of the end of your rope?" the little man pursued, grimly playful. "Give you an Inche and—what will you take, eh?"

With an inarticulate cry, Shaynon's fist shot out as if to strike his persecutor down; but in mid-air P. Sybarite's slim, strong fingers closed round and inflexibly stayed his enemy's wrist, with barely perceptible effort swinging it down and slewing the man off poise, so that perforce he staggered back against the stone of the window's deep embrasure.

"Behave!" P. Sybarite counselled evenly. "Remember where you are—in a lady's presence. Do you want to go sprawling from the sole of my foot into the presence of more than one— or over this railing, to the sidewalk, and become food for inch-worms?"

Releasing Shaynon, he stepped back warily, anticipating nothing less than an instant and disgraceful brawl.

"As for my mask," he said—"if it still annoys you—"

He jerked it off and away.

Escaping the balustrade, it caught a wandering air and drifted indolently down through the darkness of the street, like an errant petal plucked from some strange and sinister bloom of scarlet violence.

"And if my face tells you nothing," he added hotly, "perhaps my name will help. It's Sybarite. You may have heard it!"

As if from a blow, Shaynon's eyes winced. Breathing heavily, he averted a face that took on the hue of parchment in the cold light striking up from the electric globes that march Fifth Avenue. Then quietly adjusting his crumpled cuff, he drew himself up.

"Marian," he said as soon as he had his voice under control, "since you wish it, I'll wait for you in the lobby, downstairs. As—as for you, sir—"

"Yes, I know," the little man interrupted wearily: "you'll 'deal with' me later, 'at a time and a place more fitting.'...Well, I won't mind the delay if you'll just trot along now, like a good dog—"

Unable longer to endure the lash of his mordacious wit, Shaynon turned and left them alone on the balcony.

"I'm sorry," P. Sybarite told the girl in unfeigned contrition. "Please forgive me. I've a vicious temper—the colour of my hair—and I couldn't resist the temptation to make him squirm."

"If you only knew how I despised him," she said, "you wouldn't think it necessary to excuse yourself—though I don't know yet what it's all about."

"Simply, I happen to have the whip-hand of the Shaynon conscience," returned P. Sybarite; "I happened to know that Bayard is secretly the husband of a woman notorious in New York under the name of Mrs. Jefferson Inche."

"Is that true? Dare I believe—?"

Intimations of fears inexpressibly alleviated breathed in her cry.

"I believe it."

"On what grounds? Tell me!"

"The word of the lady herself, together with the evidence of his confusion just now. What more do you need?"

Turning aside, the girl rested a hand upon the balustrade and gazed blankly off through the night.

"But—I can't help thinking there must be some mistake— some terrible mistake."

"If so, it is theirs—the Shaynons', father and son."

"But they've been bringing such pressure to bear to make me agree to an earlier wedding day—!"

"Not even that shakes my belief in Mrs. Inche's story. As a matter of fact, Bayard offered her half a million if she'd divorce him quietly, without any publicity, in the West."

"And she accepted—?"

"She has refused, believing she stands to gain more by holding on."

"If that is true, how can it be that he has been begging me this very night to marry him within a month?"

"He may have entertained hopes of gaining his end—his freedom—in another way."

"It's—it's inexpressibly horrible!" the girl cried, twisting her hands together.

"Furthermore," argued the little man, purposefully unresponsive, "he probably thinks himself forced to seem insistent by the part he's playing. His father doesn't know of this entanglement; he'd disinherit Bayard if he did; naturally, Bayard wouldn't dare to seem reluctant to hasten matters, for fear of rousing the old man's suspicions."

"It may be so," she responded vacantly, in the confusion of adjusting her vision of life to this new and blinding light....

"Tell me," he suggested presently, stammering—"if you don't mind giving me more of your confidence—to which I don't pretend to have any right—only my interest in—in you—the mystery with which you surround yourself—living alone there in that wretched boarding-house—"

He broke off with a brief uneasy laugh: "I don't seem to get anywhere.... My fear lest you think me presumptuous—"

"Don't fear that for another instant—please!" she begged earnestly; and swinging to face him again, gave him an impulsive hand. "I'm so grateful to you for—for what you've saved me from—"

"Then..." Self-distrustful, he retained her fingers only transiently. "Then why not tell me—everything. If I understood, I might be able to offer some suggestions—to save you further distress—"

"Oh, no; you can't do that," she interrupted. "If what you've said is true, I—I shall simply continue to live by myself."

"You don't mean you would go back to Thirty-eighth Street?"

"No," she said thoughtfully, "I'm—I don't mean that."

"You're right," he assured her. "It's no place for you."

"That wasn't meant to be permanent," she explained—"merely an experiment. I went there for two reasons: to be rid for a while of their incessant attempts to hasten my marriage with Bayard; and because I suddenly realised I knew nothing about my father's estate, and found I was to know nothing for another year—that is, until, under his will, I come into my fortune. Old Mr. Shaynon would tell me nothing—treated me as though I were still a child. Moreover I had grown deeply interested in the way our girls were treated; I wanted to know about them—to be sure they were given a fair chance—earned enough to live decently—and other things about their lives—you can imagine...."

"I think I understand," said P. Sybarite gravely.

"I had warned them more than once I'd run away if they didn't let me alone.... You see, Mr. Shaynon insisted it was my father's wish that I should marry Bayard, and on that understanding I promised to marry him when I came into possession of the estate. But that didn't suit—or rather, it seemed to satisfy them only for a little time. Very soon they were pestering me again to marry at once. I couldn't see the need—and finally I kept my word and ran away—took my room in Thirty-eighth Street, and before long secured work in my own store. At first I was sure they'd identify me immediately; but somehow no one seemed to suspect me, and I stayed on, keeping my eyes open and collecting evidence of a system of mismanagement and oppression—but I can't talk about that calmly—"

"Please don't if it distresses you," P. Sybarite begged gently.

"At all events," she resumed, "it wasn't until to-night that Bayard found out where I was living—as you saw. At first I refused to return home, but he declared my disappearance was creating a scandal; that one newspaper threatened to print a story about my elopement with a chauffeur, and that there was other unpleasant talk about Mr. Shaynon's having caused me to be spirited away so that he might gain control of my estate—"

"Wonder what put *that* into his head!" P. Sybarite broke in with quickening curiosity.

"He insisted that these stories could only be refuted if I'd come home for a few days and show myself at this dance to-night. And when I still hesitated, he threatened—"

"What?" growled the little man.

"That, if I didn't consent, he'd telephone the paper to go ahead and publish that awful story about the chauffeur."

P. Sybarite caught himself barely in time to shut his teeth upon an expletive.

"There!" said the girl. "Don't let's talk about it any longer. After what you've told me.... Well, it's all over now!"

P. Sybarite pondered this in manifest doubt.

"Are you sure?" he queried with his head thoughtfully to one side.

"Am I sure?" she repeated, puzzled. "Rather! I tell you, I've finished with the Shaynons for good and all. I never liked either of them—never understood what father saw in old Mr. Shaynon to make him trust him the way he did. And now, after what has happened ... I shall stop at the Plaza to-night— they know me there—and telephone for my things. If Mr. Shaynon objects, I'll see if the law won't relieve me of his guardianship."

"If you'll take a fool's advice, you'll do that, whether or no. An uneasy conscience is a fine young traitor to its possessor, as a rule."

"Now, what can you mean by that?"

"I don't believe there's been any whisper of suspicion that the Shaynons had caused you to be spirited away."

"Then why did Bayard say—"

"Because he was thinking about it! The unconscious self-betrayal of the unskilled but potential criminal."

"Oh!" cried the girl in horror. "I don't think *that*—"

"Well, I do," said P. Sybarite gloomily. "I know they're capable of it. It wouldn't be the first time Brian Shaynon ruined a friend. There was once a family in this town by the name of Sybarite—the family of a rich and successful man, associated with Brian Shaynon in a business way. I'm what's left of it, thanks to *my* father's faith in old Brian's integrity. It's too long a story to detail; but the old fox managed to keep within the letter of the law when he robbed me of my inheritance, and there's no legal way to get back at him. I'm telling you all this only to show you how far the man's to be trusted."

"Oh, I'm sorry—!"

"Don't be, please. What I've endured has done me no harm—and to-night has seen the turn of my fortunes—or else I'm hopelessly deluded. Furthermore, some day I mean to square my account with Brian Shaynon to the fraction of a penny—and within the law."

"Oh, I do hope you may!"

P. Sybarite smiled serenely. "I shall; and you can help me, if you will."

"How?"

"Stick to your resolution to have no more to do with the family; retain a good lawyer to watch your interests under old Brian's charge; and look out for yourself."

"I'll surely do all that, Mr. Sybarite; but I don't understand—"

"Well, if I'm not mistaken, it'll help a lot. Public disavowal of your engagement to Bayard will be likely to bring Shaynon's affairs to a crisis. I firmly believe they're hard pressed for money—that it wasn't consolidation of two going-concerns for mutual advantage, but the finding of new capital for a moribund and insolvent house that they've been seeking through this marriage. That's why they were in such a hurry. Even if Bayard were free—as his father believes him to be—why need the old man have been so unreasonable when all the delay you ask is another twelvemonth? Believe me, he had some excellent reason for his anxiety. Finally, if the old villain isn't fomenting some especially foul villainy, why need he sneak from here to-night to the lowest dive in town to meet and confer with a gang leader and murderer like Red November?"

"What are you talking about now?" demanded the bewildered girl.

"An hour or so ago I met old Brian coming out of a dive known as Dutch House, the worst in this old Town. What business had he there, if he's an honest man? I can't tell you because I don't know. But it was foul—that's certain. Else why need he have incited Red and his followers to drug Peter Kenny into forgetfulness? Peter found him there before I did. It was only after the deuce of a row that I got the boy away alive."

Temporarily he suppressed mention of Peter's hurt. The girl had enough to occupy her without being subjected to further drain upon her sympathies.

"I'd like to know!" he wound up gloomily.... "That old scoundrel never visited Dutch House out of simple curiosity; and whatever his purpose, one thing's sure—it wasn't one to stand daylight. It's been puzzling me ever since—an appointment of some sort he made with November just as I hove within earshot. '*Two-thirty*,' he said; and November repeated the hour and promised to be on the job. 'Two-thirty!'—what *can* it mean? It's later than that now but—mark my words!—something's going to happen this afternoon, or to-morrow, or some time soon, at half-past two o'clock!"

"Perhaps you're right," said the girl doubtfully. "And yet you may be wrong in thinking me involved in any way. Indeed, I'm sure you must be wrong. I can't believe that he could wish me actual harm."

"Miss Blessington," said P. Sybarite solemnly, "when you ran off in that taxi at midnight, I had five dollars in all the world. This minute, as I stand, I'm worth twenty-five thousand— more money than I ever hoped to see in this life. It means a lot to me—a start toward independence—but I'd give every cent of it for some reliable assurance that Brian Shaynon and his son mean you no harm."

Surprised and impressed by his unwonted seriousness, the girl instinctively shrank back against the balustrade.

"Mr. Sybarite—!" she murmured, wide-eyed.

He remarked her action with a gesture almost of supplication.

"Don't be alarmed," he begged; and there was in his voice the least flavour of bitterness. "I'm not going to say anything I shouldn't—anything you wouldn't care to hear. I'm not altogether mad, Miss Blessington; only...

"Well!" he laughed quietly—"when my run of luck set in to-night back there at the gambling house, I told myself it was *Kismet's* doing—that this was my Day of Days. If I had thought, I should instead have called it my Night of Nights—knowing it must wear out with the dawn."

His gesture drew her heed to the east; where, down the darkling, lamp-studded canyon of a cross-town street, stark against a sky pulsing with the faintest foreboding of daybreak, the gaunt, steel-girdered framework of the new Grand Central Station stood—in its harshly angular immensity as majestic as the blackened skeleton of a burnt-out world glimpsed against the phosphorescent pallor of the last chill dawn....

In the great ball-room behind them, the last strains of dance music were dying out.

"Now," said the little man with a brisker accent, "by your leave, we get back to what we were discussing; your welfare—"

"Mr. Sybarite," the girl interrupted impetuously—"whatever happens, I want you to know that I at least understand you; and that to me you'll always be my standard of a gentleman brave and true—and kind."

As impulsively as she had spoken, she gave him her hands.

Holding them fugitively in both his own, he gazed intently into the shadowed loveliness of her face.

Then with a slight shake of his head—whether of renunciation or of disappointment, she couldn't tell—he bent so low that for a thought she fancied he meant to touch his lips to her fingers.

But he gave them back to her as they had come to him.

"It is you who are kind, Miss Blessington," he said steadily— "very kind indeed to me. I presume, and you permit; I violate your privacy, and you are not angry; I am what I am—and you are kind. That is going to be my most gracious memory...

"And now," he broke off sharply, "all the pretty people are going home, and you must, too. May I venture one step farther? Don't permit Bayard Shaynon—"

"I don't mean to," she told him. "Knowing what I know—it's impossible."

"You will go to the Plaza?"

"Yes," she replied: "I've made up my mind to that."

"You have a cab waiting, of course. May I call it for you?"

"My own car," she said; "the call check is with my wraps. But," she smiled, "I shall be glad to give it to you, to hand to the porter, if you'll be so good."

He had longed to be asked to accompany her; and at the same time prayed to be spared that trial. Already he had ventured too perilously close to the brink of open avowal of his heart's desire. And that way—well he knew it!—humiliation lay, and opaque despair. Better to live on in the melancholy company of a hopeless heart than in the wretchedness of one rejected and despised. And who—and what—was he, that she should look upon him with more than the transient favour of pity or of gratitude for a service rendered?

But, since she, wise in her day and generation, did not ask him, suddenly he was glad. The tension of his emotion eased. He even found grace to grin amiably.

"To do Bayard out of that honour!" he said cheerfully. "You couldn't invent a service to gratify me more hugely."

She smiled in sympathy.

"But he will be expecting to see you home?"

"No matter if he does, he shan't. Besides, he lives in bachelor rooms—within walking distance, I believe."

Holding aside the window draperies, he followed her through to the ball-room.

Already the vast and shining hall was almost empty; only at the farther wall a handful of guests clustered round the doorway, waiting to take their turn in the crowded cloakrooms. Off to one side, in a deep apsidal recess, the members of the orchestra were busily packing up their instruments. And as the last of the guests—save Marian Blessington and P. Sybarite—edged out into the ante-rooms, a detachment of servants invaded the dancing-floor and bustled about setting the room to rights.

A moment more, and the two were close upon the vanguard of departing guests.

"You'll have a time finding your hat and coat," smiled the girl.

"I? Not I. With marvellous sagacity, I left 'em with a waiter downstairs. But you?"

"I'm afraid I must keep you waiting. No matter if it is four in the morning—and later—women do take a time to wrap up.

You won't mind?"

"Not in the least—it prolongs my Day of Days!" he laughed.

"I shall look for you in the lobby," she replied, smiling; and slipped away through the throng.

Picking his way to the elevators, constantly squirming more inextricably into the heart of the press, elbowed and shouldered and politely walked upon, not only fore and aft, but to port and starboard as well, by dame, dowager, and debutante, husband, lover, and esquire, patricians, celebrities and the commonalty (a trace, as the chemists say), P. Sybarite at length found himself only a layer or two removed from the elevator gates.

And one of these presently opening, he stumbled in with the crush, to hold his breath in vain effort to make himself smaller, gaze in cross-eyed embarrassment at the abundant and nobly undisguised back of the lady of distinction in front of him, and stand on tiptoes to spare those of the man behind him; while the cage descended with maddening deliberation.

If he had but guessed the identity of the man in the rear, the chances are he would have (thoughtlessly of course) brought down his heels upon the other's toes with all his weight on top of them. But in his ignorance P. Sybarite was diligent to keep the peace.

Liberated on the lower floor, he found his lackey, resumed hat and coat, and mounted guard in the lobby opposite the elevators.

Miss Blessington procrastinating consistently with her warning, he schooled himself to patience, mildly diverted by inspection of those who passed him, going out.

At the side-street entrance, the crush of ante-room and elevators was duplicated, people jamming the doorway and overflowing to the sidewalk while awaiting their motor-cars and carriages.

But through the Fifth Avenue entrance only the thin stream of those intending to walk was trickling away.

After a time P. Sybarite discovered Mr. Bayard Shaynon not far off, like himself waiting and with a vigilant eye reviewing the departing, the while he talked in close confidence with one who, a stranger to P. Sybarite, was briefly catalogued in his gallery of impressions as "hard-faced, cold-eyed, middle-aged, fine-trained but awkward—very likely, *nouveau riche*;" and with this summary, dismissed from the little man's thoughts.

When idly he glanced that way a second time, the younger Shaynon was alone, and had moved nearer; his countenance impassive, he looked through and beyond P. Sybarite a thought too ostentatiously. But when eventually Marian appeared, he was instant to her side, forestalling even the alert flanking movement of P. Sybarite.

"You're quite ready, Marian?" Shaynon asked; and familiarly slipped a guiding hand beneath the arm of the girl—with admirable effrontery ignoring his earlier dismissal.

On the instant, halting, the girl turned to him a full, cold stare.

"I prefer you do not touch me," she said clearly, yet in low tones.

"Oh, come!" he laughed uneasily. "Don't be foolish—"

"Did you hear me, Bayard?"

"You're making a scene—" the man flashed, colouring darkly.

"And," P. Sybarite interjected quietly, "I'll make it worse if you don't do as Miss Blessington bids you."

With a shrug, Shaynon removed his hand; but with no other acknowledgment of the little man's existence, pursued indulgently: "You have your carriage-call check ready, Marian? If you'll let me have it—"

"Let's understand one another, once and for all time, Bayard," the girl interrupted. "I don't wish you to take me home. I prefer to go alone. Is that clear? I don't wish to feel indebted to you for even so slight a service as this," she added, indicating the slip of pasteboard in her fingers. "But if Mr. Sybarite will be so kind—"

The little man accepted the card with no discernible sign of jubilation over Shaynon's discomfiture.

"Thank you," he said mildly; but waited close by her side.

For a moment Shaynon's face reminded him of one of the masks of crimson lacquer and black that grinned from the walls of Mrs. Inche's "den." But his accents, when he spoke, were even, if menacing in their tonelessness.

"Then, Marian, I'm to understand it's—goodnight?"

"I think," said the girl with a level look of disdain, "it might be far better if you were to understand that it's good-bye."

"You," he said with slight difficulty—"you mean that, Marian?"

"Finally!" she asseverated.

He shrugged again; and his eyes, wavering, of a sudden met P. Sybarite's and stabbed them with a glance of ruthless and unbridled hatred, so envenomed that the little man was transiently conscious of a misgiving.

"Here," he told himself in doubt, "is one who, given his way, would have me murdered within twenty-four hours!"

And he thought of Red November, and wondered what had been the fate of that personage at the hands of the valiant young patrolman. Almost undoubtedly the gunman had escaped arrest....

Shaynon had turned and was striding away toward the Fifth Avenue entrance, when Marian roused P. Sybarite with a word.

"Finis," she said, enchanting him with the frank intimacy of her smile.

He made, with a serious visage, the gesture of crossed fingers that exorcises an evil spirit.

"*Absit omen!*" he muttered, with a dour glance over shoulder at the retreating figure of his mortal enemy.

"Why," she laughed incredulously, "you're not afraid?"

Forcing a wry grin, he mocked a shudder.

"Some irreverent body walked over the grave of me."

"You're superstitious!"

"I'm Irish," P. Sybarite explained sufficiently.

XVIII

THE BROOCH

They came to the carriage entrance, where the crush of waiting people had somewhat thinned—not greatly.

Leaving Marian in the angle of the doorway, P. Sybarite pressed out to the booth of the carriage-call apparatus, gave the operator the numbered and perforated cardboard together with a coin, saw the man place it on the machine and shoot home a lever that hissed and spat blue fire; then turned back.

"What was the number?" she asked as he approached. "Did you notice? I did—but then thought of something else; and now I've forgotten."

"Two hundred and thirty," replied P. Sybarite absently.

Between the two there fell a little pause of constrained silence ended by Marian.

"I want to see you again, very soon, Mr. Sybarite."

The eyes of the little man were as grateful as a dog's.

"If I may call—?" he ventured diffidently.

"Could you come to-morrow to tea?"

"At the Plaza?"

"At the Plaza!" she affirmed with a bright nod.

"Thank you."

Above the hum of chattering voices rose the bellow of the carriage porter:

"Two hundred and thirty! *Two* hundred and *thirty*!"

"My car!" said the girl with a start.

P. Sybarite moved in front of her, signalling with a lifted hand.

"Two hundred and thirty," he repeated.

A handsome town-car stood at the curb beneath the permanent awning of iron and glass. Behind it a long rank waited with impatient, stuttering motors and dull-burning lamps that somehow forced home drowsy thoughts of bed.

Hurrying across the sidewalk, Marian permitted P. Sybarite to help her into the vehicle.

Transported by this proof of her graciousness, he gave the chauffeur the address:

"Hotel Plaza."

With the impudent imperturbability of his breed, the man nodded and grunted without looking round.

From the body of the vehicle Marian extended a white-gloved hand.

"Good-night, Mr. Sybarite. To-morrow—at five."

Touching her fingers, P. Sybarite raised his hat; but before he could utter the response ready upon his tongue, he was seized by the arm and swung rudely away from the door. At the same time a voice (the property of the owner of that unceremonious hand) addressed the porter roughly:

"Shut that door and send the car along! I'll take charge of this gentleman!"

In this speech an accent of irony inhered to exasperate P. Sybarite. Half a hundred people were looking on—listening! Angrily he wrenched his arm free.

"What the devil—!" he cried into the face of the aggressor; and in the act of speaking, recognised the man as him with whom Bayard Shaynon had been conversing in the lobby: that putative parvenu—hard-faced, cold-eyed, middle-aged, fine-trained, awkward in evening dress....

The hand whose grasp he had broken shifted to his shoulder, closing fingers like steel hooks upon it.

"If you need a row," the man advised him quietly, "try that again. If you've got good sense—come along quiet'."

"Where? What for? What right have you—?" P. Sybarite demanded in one raging breath.

"I'm the house detective here," the other answered, holding his eyes with an inexorable glare. And the muscles of his heavy jaw tightened even as he tightened his grasp upon the little man's shoulder. "And if it's all the same to you, we're going to have a quiet little talk in the office," he added with a jerk of his head.

A sidelong glance discovered the fact that Marian's car had disappeared. Doubtless she had gone in ignorance of this outrage, perhaps thinking him accosted by a chance acquaintance. At all events, she was gone, and there was now nothing to be gained from an attempt to bluster the detective down, but deeper shame and the scorn of all beholders.

"What do you want?" the little man asked in a more pacific tone.

"We can talk better inside, unless"—the detective grinned sardonically—"you want to get out hand-bills about this matter."

"Let me go, then," said P. Sybarite. "I'll follow you."

"You've got a better guess than that: you'll go ahead of me," retorted the other. "And while you're doing it, remember that there's a cop at the Fifth Avenue door, and I've got a handy little emergency ration in my pocket—with my hand on the butt of it."

"Very well," said P. Sybarite, boiling with rage beneath thin ice of submission.

His shoulder free, he moved forward with a high chin and a challenge in his eye for any that dared question his burning face—marched up the steps through ranks that receded as if to escape pollution, and so re-entered the lobby.

"Straight ahead," admonished his captor, falling in at his side. "First door to the right of the elevators."

Shoulder to shoulder, the target for two-score grinning or surprised stares, they strode across the lobby and through the designated door.

It was immediately closed; and the key, turned in the lock, was removed and pocketed by the detective.

In this room—a small interior apartment, plainly furnished as a private office—two people were waiting: a stout, smooth little man with a moustache of foreign extraction, who on better acquaintance proved to be the manager of the establishment; the other Bayard Shaynon, stationed with commendable caution on the far side of the room, the bulk of

Louis Joseph Vance

a broad, flat-topped mahogany desk fencing him off from the wrathful little captive.

"Well?" this last demanded of the detective the moment they were private.

"Take it calm', son, take it calm'," counselled the man, his tone not altogether lacking in good-nature. "There seems to be some question as to your right to attend that party upstairs; we got to investigate you, for the sake of the rep. of the house. Get me?"

P. Sybarite drew a long breath. If this were all that Shaynon could have trumped up to discomfit him—! He looked that one over with the curling lip of contempt.

"I believe it's no crime to enter where you've not been invited, provided you don't force door or window to do it," he observed.

"You admit—eh?" the manager broke in excitedly—"you have no card of invitation, what?"

"I freely admit I have no card of invitation what or whatever."

"Then perhaps you'll explain whatcha doing here," suggested the detective, not without affability.

"Willingly: I came to find a friend—a lady whose name I don't care to bring into this discussion—unless Mr. Shaynon has forestalled me."

"Mr. Shaynon has mentioned a lady's name," said the manager with a significance lost upon P. Sybarite.

"That," he commented acidly, "is much what might have been expected of'—here he lifted his shoulders with admirable insolence—"Mr. Shaynon."

"You saw this lady, then?" the detective put in sharply.

"Why—yes," P. Sybarite admitted.

"He not only saw her," Shaynon interpolated with a malicious sneer, "but I saw him see her—and saw him get away with it."

"Get away with—what?" P. Sybarite asked blankly.

"Mr. Shaynon," drawled the detective, "says he saw you lift a di'mond brooch off'n Mrs. Addison Strone, while you was in the elevator."

And while P. Sybarite gaped, thunderstruck and breathless with the rage excited by this groundless accusation, the detective looked to Shaynon for confirmation.

"I stood behind him in the elevator, coming down, ten minutes or so ago," the latter stated heavily. "Mrs. Addison Strone was immediately in front of him. The cage was badly crowded—no one could move. But practically every one else was with friends, you understand—laughing, talking, paying no attention to this—ah—creature. As I got in, I noticed that Mrs. Strone's brooch, a gold bar set with several large diamonds, was apparently loose—pin had parted from the catch, you know—and meant to warn her she was in danger of losing it; but I couldn't, without shouting over this fellow's head, so waited until we got out; and then, when I managed to get to her, the brooch was gone. Later, I remembered this— fellow—and looking round the lobby, saw him in a corner, apparently concealing something about his person. So I spoke to you about it."

P. Sybarite's face settled into grim lines. "Shaynon," he said slowly, without visible temper, "this won't get you anything but trouble. Remember that, when I come to pay you out— unless you'll have the grace to retract here and now."

As if he had not heard, Shaynon deliberately produced a gold case, supplied himself with a cigarette, and lighted it.

"Meanin', I take it," the detective interpolated, "you plead not guilty?"

P. Sybarite nodded curtly. "It's a lie, out of whole cloth," he declared. "You've only to search me. I'm not strong for that—mind—and I'm going to make the lot of you smart for this indignity; but I'm perfectly willing to prove my innocence now, by letting you search me, so long as it affords me an earlier opportunity to catch Mister Shaynon when he hasn't got you to protect him."

"That's big talk," commended the detective, apparently a little prepossessed; "and it's all to the good if you can back it up." He rose. "You don't mind my going through your pockets—sure?"

"Go ahead," P. Sybarite told him shortly.

"To save time," Shaynon suggested dispassionately, "you might explore his coat-tail pockets first. It was there that I saw him put away the brooch."

Nervously in his indignation, P. Sybarite caught his coat-tails from beneath his Inverness, dragged them round in front of him, and fumbling, found a pocket.

Groping therein, his fingers brushed something strange to him—a small, hard, and irregular body which, escaping his clutches, fell with a soft thud to the carpet at his feet.

Transfixed, he stared down, and gulped with horror, shaken by a sensation little short of nausea, as he recognised in the object—a bar of yellow metal studded with winking brilliants of considerable size—the brooch described by Shaynon.

With a noncommittal grunt, the detective stooped and retrieved this damning bit of evidence, while the manager moved quickly to his side, to inspect the find. And P. Sybarite looked up with blank eyes in a pallid, wizened face in time to see Shaynon bare his teeth—his lips curling back in a manner peculiarly wolfish and irritating—and snarl a mirthless laugh.

It was something inopportune; the man could have done no better than keep his peace; left to himself P. Sybarite would in all probability have floundered and blustered and committed himself inextricably in a multitude of hasty and ill-considered protestations.

But that laugh was as good as a douche of cold water in his face. He came abruptly to his senses; saw clearly how this thing had come to pass: the temptation of the loose brooch to Shaynon's fingers itching for revenge, while they stood so near together in the elevator, the opportunity grasped with the avidity of low cunning, the brooch transferred, under cover of the crush, to the coat-tail pocket.

Mute in this limpid comprehension of the circumstances, he sobered thoroughly from sickening consternation; remained in his heart a foul sediment of deadly hatred for Shaynon; to whom he nodded with a significance that wiped the grimace from the man's face as with a sponge. Something clearly akin to fear informed Shaynon's eyes. He sat forward with an uneasy glance at the door.

And then P. Sybarite smiled sunnily in the face of the detective.

"Caught with the goods on, eh?" he chirped.

"Well," growled the man, dashed. "Now, what do *you* think?"

"I'm every bit as much surprised as you are," P. Sybarite confessed. "Come now—be fair to me—own up: you didn't expect to see that—did you?"

The detective hesitated. "Well," he grudged, "you did have me goin' for a minute—you were so damn' cock-sure—and it certainly is pretty slick work for an amateur."

"You think I'm an amateur—eh?"

"I guess I know every map in the Rogues' Gallery as well's the palm of my hand!"

"And mine is not among them?" P. Sybarite insisted triumphantly.

The detective grunted disdain of this inconclusive argument: "You all've got to begin. It'll be there to-morrow, all right."

"It looks bad, eh—not?" the manager questioned, his predacious eyes fixed greedily upon the trinket.

"You think so?" P. Sybarite purposefully misinterpreted. "Let me see."

Before the detective could withdraw, P. Sybarite caught the brooch from his fingers.

"Bad?" he mused aloud, examining it closely. "Phony? Perhaps it is. Looks like *Article de Paris* to me. See what you think."

He returned the trinket indifferently.

"Nonsense!" Shaynon interposed incisively. "Mrs. Strone's not that kind."

"Shut up!" snapped P. Sybarite. "What do you know about it? You've lied yourself out of court already."

A transitory expression of bewilderment clouded Shaynon's eyes.

"I'm no judge," the detective announced doubtfully.

"It makes no difference," Shaynon insisted. "Theft's theft!"

"It makes a deal of difference whether it's grand or petit larceny," P. Sybarite flashed—"a difference almost as wide and deep as that which yawns between attempted and successful wife-murder, Mr. Shaynon!"

His jaw dropped and a look of stupefying terror stamped itself upon Shaynon's face.

It was the turn of P. Sybarite to laugh.

"Well?" he demanded cuttingly. "Are you ready to come to the station-house and make a charge against me? I'll go peaceful as a lamb with the kind cop, if by so doing I can take you with me. But if I do, believe me, you'll never get out without a bondsman."

Shaynon recollected himself with visible effort.

"The man's crazy," he muttered sickishly, rising. "I don't know what he's talking about. Arrest him—take him to the station-house—why don't you?"

"Who'll make the charge?" asked the detective, eyeing Shaynon without favour.

"Not Bayard Shaynon!" P. Sybarite asseverated.

"It's not my brooch," Shaynon asserted defensively.

"You saw him take it," the detective persisted.

"No—I didn't; I suspected him. It's you who found the brooch on him, and it's your duty to make the charge."

"You're one grand little lightning-change-of-heart-artist—gotta slip it to you for that," the detective observed truculently. "Now, lis'n: I don't make no charge—"

"Any employee of the establishment will do as well, for *my* purpose," P. Sybarite cut in. "Come, Mr. Manager! How about you? Mr. Shaynon declines; your detective has no stomach for the job. Suppose you take on the dirty work— kind permission of Bayard Shaynon, Esquire. I don't care, so long as I get my grounds for suit against the Bizarre."

The manager spread out expostulatory palms. "Me, I have nossing whatever to do with the matter," he protested. "To me it would seem Mrs. Strone should make the charge."

"Well?" mumbled the detective of Shaynon. "How aboutcha?"

"Wait," mumbled Shaynon, moving toward the door. "I'll fetch Mrs. Strone."

"Don't go without saying good-bye," P. Sybarite admonished him severely. "It isn't pretty manners."

The door slammed tempestuously, and the little man chuckled with an affectation of ease to which he was entirely a stranger: ceaselessly his mind was engaged with the problem of this trumped-up charge of Shaynon's.

Was simple jealousy and resentment, a desire to "get even," the whole explanation?

Or was there something of an uglier complexion at the bottom of the affair?

His head buzzed with doubts and suspicions, and with misgivings on Marian's behalf but indifferently mitigated by the reflection that, at worst, the girl had escaped unhindered and alone in her private car. By now she ought to be safe at the Plaza....

"He won't be back," P. Sybarite observed generally to detective and manager; and sat him down serenely.

"You feel pretty sure about that?" the detective asked.

"Wait and see."

Bending forward, the little man examined the gilt clock on the manager's desk. "Twenty minutes past four," he announced: "I give you ten minutes to find some one to make a charge against me—Shaynon, Mrs. What's-her-name, or either of yourselves, if you like the job. If you fail to produce a complainant by half-past four precisely, out of here I go—and I'm sorry for the man who tries to stop me."

The detective took a chair, crossed his legs, and produced a cigar which he began to trim with tender care. The manager, anxiously pacing the floor, after another moment or so paused at the door, fidgeted, jerked it open, and with a muffled "Pardon!" disappeared—presumably in search of Shaynon.

Striking a match, the detective puffed his cigar aglow. Over its tip his small eyes twinkled at P. Sybarite.

"Maybe you're a gentleman crook, and maybe not," he returned with fine impartiality. "But you're all there, son, with the tongue action. You got me still goin' round in circles. Damn'f I know yet what to think."

"Well, if that's your trouble," P. Sybarite told him coolly, "this is your cue to squat on your haunches, scratch your left ear with your hind leg, and gaze up into my face with an intelligent expression in your great brown eyes."

"I'll do better 'n that," chuckled the man. "Have a cigar."

"Thank you," said P. Sybarite politely, accepting the peace offering. "All I need now is a match: I acknowledge the habit."

The match supplied, he smoked in silence.

Four minutes passed, by the clock: no sign of the manager,

Shaynon, or Mrs. Strone.

"Story?" the detective suggested at length.

"Plant," retorted P. Sybarite as tersely.

"You mean he salted you?"

"In the elevator, of course."

"It come to me, that was the way of it when he sprung that bunk stuff about you coarsely loading said loot into your coat-tail," admitted the detective. "That didn't sound sensible, even if you did have a skirt to fuss into a cab. The ordinary vest-pocket of commerce would've kept it just as close, besides being more natural—easy to get at. Then the guy was too careful to tip me off not to pinch you until the lady had went—didn't want her name dragged into it.... A fellow in my job's gotta have a lot of imagination," he concluded complacently. "That's why I'm letting you get away with it in this unprofessional manner."

"More human than in line with the best literary precedent, eh?"

"That's me. I seen he was sore when the dame turned him down, too, and started right off wondering if maybe it wasn't a jealousy plant. I seen this sorta thing happen before. Not that I blame him for feeling cut up: that was one swell piece of goods you bundled into numba two-thirty."

P. Sybarite's cigar dropped unheeded from his lips.

"*What!*" he cried.

The detective started.

"Wasn't that the numba of the lady's cab—two-thirty?"

"Good God!" ejaculated P. Sybarite, jumping up.

"What's hit you?"

"I'm going!" the little man announced fiercely.

"Your time allowance ain't expired by several minutes—"

"To hell with my time allowance! Try to keep me, if you like!"

P. Sybarite strode excitedly to the door and jerked it open. The detective followed him, puffing philosophically.

There was no one in sight in the hall.

"Looks like you got a fine show for a clean getaway," he observed cheerfully between his teeth. "Your friend's beaten it, the boss has ducked the responsibility, and you got *me* scared to death. Besides—damn'f I'm going to be thegoat that saddles this hash-hut with a suit for damages."

His concluding words were addressed to the horizontal folds of the inverness that streamed from the shoulders of P. Sybarite as he bolted unhindered through the Fifth Avenue doorway.

XIX

NEMESIS

"Dolt!... Blockhead!... Imbecile!... Idiot!... Numskull!... Ass!... Simpleton!... Loon!..."

The chill air of early morning wiped the blistering epithets from his lips as he fled like a madman down Fifth Avenue, at every stride wringing from the depths of an embittered bosom new and more virulent terms of vituperation with which to characterize his infatuated stupidity—and finding one and all far too mild. In simple truth, the King's English lacked invective poisonous enough to do justice to his self-contempt.

Deliberately had he permitted himself to be duped, circumvented, over-reached. He had held in his hand a tangible clue to that mystery which had so perplexed him— and had allowed it to be filched away before he could recognise it and shape his course accordingly.

Why had he never for an instant dreamed that the term "*two-thirty*" could indicate anything but the hour of some otherwise undesignated appointment? Of course it had signified the number of Marian's carriage-check, "230": *two hundred and thirty*, rolling off the modern tongue, stripped to essentials— thanks to the telephone's abbreviated influence—as, simply, "*two-thirty*"!

And he had held that check in his hand, had memorised its

number and repeated it to Marian, had heard it bawled by the carriage porter, had shouted it himself in reply: never for an instant thinking to connect it with the elder Shaynon's parting admonition to the gang leader!

If he had ere this entertained any doubts whatever of the ugly grounds for his fears they were now resolved by recognition of Bayard's clumsy ruse to keep him both out of the cab and out of the way, while November and his lieutenants executed their infamous commission....

And all that was now ten—fifteen—twenty minutes old! Marian's car was gone; and if it had not reached the Plaza, the girl was lost, irrevocably lost to the frantic little man with the twinkling red heels and scarlet breeches, sprinting so wildly down Fifth Avenue in the dank, weird dusk that ran before the dawn of that April morning.

Fortunately he hadn't far to run; else he would certainly have been waylaid or overhauled by some policeman of enquiring turn of mind, anxious (in the way of duty) to learn his reason for such extraordinary haste.

As it was, P. Sybarite managed to make his goal in record time without attracting the attention of more than half a dozen wayfarers; all of whom gave him way and went their own with that complete indifference so distinctly Manhattanesque....

He had emerged from the restaurant building to find the street bare of any sort of hirable conveyance and himself in a fret too exacting to consider walking to the Plaza or taking a street-car thither. Nothing less than a taxicab—and that, one with a speed-mad chauffeur—would satisfy his impatient humour.

And indeed, if there were a grain of truth in his suspicions, formless though in a measure they remained, he had not an instant to lose.

But on the way to the Bizarre from Peter Kenny's rooms, some freak of a mind superficially preoccupied had caused him to remark, on the south side of Forty-third Street, immediately east of Sixth Avenue, a long rank of buildings which an utilitarian age had humbled from their once proud estate of private stables to the lowlier degree of quarters for motor vehicles both public and private.

Of these one building boasted the blazing electric announcement: "*ALL NIGHT GARAGE.*"

Into this last P. Sybarite pelted at the top of his speed and pulled up puffing, to stare nervously round a place gloomy, cavernous, and pungent with fragrance of oil, rubber, and gasoline. Here and there lonely electric bulbs made visible somnolent ranks of motor-cars. Out of the shadows behind him, presently, came a voice drawling:

"You certainly do take on like you'd lost a power of trouble."

P. Sybarite whirled round as if stung. The speaker occupied a chair tilted back against the wall, his feet on the rungs, a cigarette smouldering between his lips in open contempt of the regulations of the Fire Department and all other admonitions of ordinary common-sense.

"What can I do for you?" he resumed, nothing about him stirring save eyes that twinkled as they travelled from head to foot of the odd and striking figure P. Sybarite presented as *Beelzebub, Knight Errant.*

"Taxi!" the little man panted vociferously.

The other yawned and stretched. "It can't be done," he admitted fairly. "They ain't no such animal on the premises."

With a gesture P. Sybarite singled out the nearest car.

"What's that?" he demanded angrily.

Shading his eyes, the man examined it with growing wonder which presently found expression: "As I live, it's an autymobeel!"

"Damn your sense of humour!" stormed P. Sybarite. "What's the matter with that car?"

"As man to man—nothing."

"Why can't I have it?"

"Ten dollars an hour—"

"I'll take it."

"But you *asked* for a taxi," grumbled the man, rising to press a button. Whereupon a bell shrilled somewhere in the dark backwards of the establishment. "Deposit...?" he suggested, turning back.

P. Sybarite disbursed a golden double-eagle; and to the operator who, roused by the bell, presently drifted out of the shadows, gaping and rubbing his eyes, he promised a liberal tip for haste.

In two minutes he was rolling out of the garage, ensconced in the body of a luxurious and high-powered touring machine which he strongly suspected to be somebody's private car lawlessly farmed out while its owner slept.

The twilight was now stronger, if still dull and as cold as the air it coloured, rendering P. Sybarite grateful for Peter Kenny's inverness as the car surged spiritedly up the deserted avenue, its disdain for speed regulations ignored by the string of yawning peg-post cops—almost the only human beings in sight.

Town was indeed deep sunk in lethargy at that small hour; the traditional milk-wagon itself seemed to have been caught napping. With one consent residence and shop and skyscraping hotel blinked apathetically at the flying car; then once more turned and slept. Even the Bizarre had forgotten P. Sybarite—showed at least no sign of recognition as he scurried past.

A curious sense of illusion troubled the little man. The glamour of the night was gone and with it all that had lent semblance of plausibility to his incredible career; daylight forced all back into confused and distorted perspective, like the pageant of some fantastic and disordered dream uncertainly recalled long hours after waking.

As for himself, in his absurd attire and bound upon his ambiguous errand, he was all out of the picture—horribly suggestive of an addled sparrow who had stayed up all night on purpose to cheat some legitimately early bird out of a chimerical first worm....

Self-conscious and ill at ease, he presented himself to the amused inspection of the night force in the office of the Plaza, made his halting enquiry, and received the discounted assurance that Miss Blessington, though a known and valued patron of the house, was not then its guest.

Convinced, as he had been from the moment that the words "two-thirty," falling from the lips of the Bizarre's house detective, had made him alive to his terrible oversight, that this would be the outcome at the Plaza, he turned away, sobered, outwitted, and miserably at a loss to guess what next to do.

Gloomily he paused with a hand on the open door of his car, thoughts profoundly disturbed and unsettled, for so long that the operator grew restless.

"Where next, sir?" he asked.

"Wait," said P. Sybarite in a manner of abstraction that did him no injustice; and entering the car, mechanically shut the door and sat down, permitting his gaze to range absently among the dusky distances of Central Park; where through the netted, leafless branches, the lamps that march the winding pathways glimmered like a hundred tiny moons of gold lost in some vast purple well....

Should he appeal to the police? His solicitude for the girl forbade him such recourse save as a last resort. Publicity must be avoided until the time when, all else having failed, it alone held out some little promise of assistance.

But—adrift and blind upon uncharted seas of uncertainty!— what to do?

Suddenly it became plain to him that if in truth it was with her as he feared, at least two persons knew what had become of the girl—two persons aside from himself and her hired kidnappers: Brian Shaynon and Bayard, his son.

From them alone authoritative information might be extracted, by ruse or wile or downright intimidation, eked out with effrontery, a stout heart, and perhaps a little luck.

A baleful light informing his eyes, an ominous expression settling about his mouth, he gave the operator the address of Shaynon's town-house; and as the car slipped away from the hotel was sensible of keen regret that he had left at Peter Kenny's, what time he changed his clothing, the pistol given him by Mrs. Jefferson Inche, together with the greater part of his fortuitous fortune—neither firearms nor large amounts of money seeming polite additions to one's costume for a dance....

In five minutes the car drew up in front of one of those few old-fashioned, brownstone, English-basement residences which to-day survive on Fifth Avenue below Fifty-ninth Street, elbowed, shouldered, and frowned down upon by beetling hives of trade.

At all of its wide, old-style windows, ruffled shades of straw-coloured silk were drawn. One sign alone held out any promise that all within were not deep in slumber: the outer front doors were not closed. Upon the frosted glass panels of the inner doors a dim light cast a sickly yellow stain.

Laying hold of an obsolete bell-pull, P. Sybarite yanked it with a spirit in tune with his temper. Immediately, and considerably to his surprise, the doors were thrown open and on the threshold a butler showed him a face of age, grey with the strain of a sleepless night, and drawn and set with bleary eyes.

"Mr. Shaynon?" the little man demanded sharply.

"W'ich Mr. Shaynon, sir?" enquired the butler, too weary to betray surprise—did he feel any—at this ill-timed call.

"Either—I don't care which."

"Mr. Bayard Shaynon 'as just left—not five minutes ago, sir."

"Left for where?"

"His apartments, I presume, sir."

"Then I'll see Mr. Brian Shaynon."

The butler's body filled the doorway. Nor did he offer to budge.

"I'm afraid, sir, Mr. Shaynon is 'ardly likely to see any one at this hour."

"He'll see me," replied P. Sybarite grimly. "He hasn't gone to bed, I gather?"

"Not yet, sir; but 'e's goin' immediate'."

"Very well. You may as well let me in."

Suspicious but impressed, the servant shuffled aside, and P. Sybarite brushed past him into the hallway.

"Where is he?"

"If you'll give me your nime, sir, I'll tell him you're 'ere."

P. Sybarite hesitated. He was in anything but the mood for joking, yet a certain dour humour in the jest caught his fancy and persuaded him against his better judgment.

"Nemesis," he said briefly.

"Mr.—name—what? Beg pardon, sir!"

"Nem-e-sis," P. Sybarite articulated distinctly. "And don't Mister it. He'll understand."

"Thenk you," muttered the servant blankly; and turned.

"If he doesn't—tell him it's the gentleman who was not masked at the Bizarre to-night."

"Very good, sir."

The man moved off toward the foot of a broad, shallow staircase at the back of the hall.

On impulse, P. Sybarite strode after him.

"On second thoughts, you needn't announce me. I'll go up with you."

"I'm afraid I can't permit that, sir," observed the butler, horrified.

"Afraid you'll have to."

And P. Sybarite would have pushed past, but the man with a

quick and frightened movement of agility uncommon in one of his age and bulk put himself in the way.

"Please, sir!" he begged. "If I was to permit that, sir, it might cost me my position."

"Well—"

P. Sybarite drew back, relenting.

But at this juncture, from a point directly over their heads, the voice of Brian Shaynon himself interrupted them.

"Who is that, Soames?" he called impatiently, without making himself immediately visible. "Has Mr. Bayard returned?"

"No, sir," the butler called, distressed. "It's—it's a person, sir—insists on seein' you—says 'is nime's Nemmysis."

"*What!*"

"He has it right—Nemesis," P. Sybarite replied incisively. "And you may as well see me now, whether you want to or not. Sooner or later you'll have to!"

There was a sound of heavy, dragging footsteps on the upper landing, and Brian Shaynon showed himself at the head of the stairs; now without his furred great-coat, but still in the evening dress of elderly Respectability—Respectability sadly rumpled and maltreated, the white shield of his bosom no longer lustrous and immaculate, his tie twisted wildly beneath one ear, his collar unbuttoned, as though wrenched from its fastenings in a moment of fury. These things apart, he had within the hour aged ten years in the flesh: gone the proud flush of his bewhiskered gills, in its place leaden pallor; and gone the quick, choleric fire from eyes now smouldering, dull and all but lifeless....

He stood peering down, with an obvious lack of recognition

that hinted at failing sight.

"I don't seem to know you," he said slowly, with a weary shake of his head; "and it's most inopportune—the hour. I fear you must excuse me."

"That can't be," P. Sybarite returned. "I've business with you—important. Perhaps you didn't catch the name I gave your butler—Nemesis."

"Nemesis?" Shaynon repeated vacantly. He staggered and descended a step before a groping hand checked him on the baluster-rail. "Nemesis! Is this an untimely joke of some sort, sir?"

His accents quavered querulously; and P. Sybarite with a flash of scorn put his unnatural condition down to drink.

"Far from it," he retorted ruthlessly. "The cat's out, my friend—your bag lean and flapping emptiness! What," he demanded sternly—"what have you done with Marian Blessington?"

"Mar—Marian?" the old voice iterated. "Why, she"—the man pulled himself together with a determined effort—"she's in her room, of course. Where should she be?"

"Is that true?" P. Sybarite demanded of the butler in a manner so peremptory that the truth slipped out before the fellow realised it.

"Miss Marian 'asn't returned as yet from the ball," he whispered. "E—'e's not quite 'imself, sir. 'E's 'ad a bit of a shock, as one might s'y. I'd go easy on 'im, if you'll take a word from me."

But P. Sybarite traversed his advice without an instant's consideration.

"Brian Shaynon," he called, "you lie! The police have caught Red November; they'll worm the truth out of him within twenty minutes, if I don't get it from you now. The game's up. Come! What have you done with the girl?"

For all answer, a low cry, like the plaint of a broken-hearted child, issued from the leaden, writhen lips of the old man.

And while he stared in wonder, Brian Shaynon seemed suddenly to lose the strength of his limbs. His legs shook beneath him as with a palsy; and then, knees buckling, he tottered and plunged headlong from top to bottom of the staircase.

XX

NOVEMBER

"E's gone," the butler announced.

Kneeling beside the inert body of Brian Shaynon, where it had lodged on a broad, low landing three steps from the foot of the staircase, he turned up to P. Sybarite fishy, unemotional eyes in a pasty fat face.

The little man said nothing.

Resting a hand on the newel-post, he looked down unmoved upon the mortal wreck of him who had been his life's bane. Brian Shaynon lay in death without majesty; a crumpled and dishevelled ruin of flesh and clothing, its very insentience suggesting to the morbid fancy of the little Irishman something foul and obscene. Brian Shaynon living had been to him a sight less intolerable....

"Dead," the butler affirmed, releasing the pulseless leaden wrist, and rising. "I presume I'd best call 'is doctor, 'adn't I, sir?"

P. Sybarite nodded indifferently. Profound thought enwrapped him like a mantle.

The butler lingered, the seals of professional reticence broken by this strange and awful accident. But there was no real emotion in his temper—only curiosity, self-interest, the impulse of loquacity.

"Stroke," he observed thoughtfully, fingering his pendulous jowls and staring; "that's w'at it was—a stroke, like. He'd 'ad a bit of shock before you come in, sir."

"Yes?" murmured P. Sybarite absently.

"Yes, sir; a bit of a shock, owin' to 'is 'avin' quarrelled with Mr. Bayard, sir."

"Oh!" P. Sybarite roused. "Quarrelled with his son, you say?"

"Yes, sir; somethin' dreadful they was goin' on. 'E couldn't 'ave got over it when you come. Mr. Bayard 'adn't been gone, not more than five minutes, sir."

P. Sybarite interrogated with his eyes alone.

"It was a bit odd, come to think of it—the 'ole affair, sir. Must 'ave been over an hour ago, Mr. Shaynon 'ere, 'e come 'ome alone from the dance—I see you must've been there yourself, sir, if I m'y mike so bold as to tike notice of your costume. Very fawncy it is, too, sir—becomes your style 'andsome, it does, sir."

"Never mind me. What happened when Mr. Shaynon came home?"

"W'y, 'e 'adn't more than got inside the 'ouse, sir, w'en a lidy called on 'im—a lidy as I'ad never set eyes on before, sime as in your caise, sir; although I wouldn't 'ave you think I mean she was of your clawss, sir. 'Ardly. Properly speakin', she wasn't a lidy at all—but a woman. I mean to s'y, a bit flash."

"I understand you. Go on."

"Well, sir, I didn't 'ave a chance to over'ear w'at 'er business were, but it seemed to work on Mr. Brian there somethin' 'orrid. They was closeted in the library upstairs not more than twenty minutes, and then she went, and 'e rung for me and to bring 'im brandy and not delay about it. 'E nearly emptied the decanter, too, before Mr. Bayard got 'ere. And the minute they come together, it was 'ammer-and-tongs. 'Ot *and* 'eavy they 'ad it for upwards of an *hour*, be'ind closed doors, sime as like with the lidy. But w'en Mr. Bayard, 'e come to go, sir, the old gent follows 'im to the landin'—just where 'e was when he spoke to you, sir, before 'e 'ad the stroke—and 'e says to 'im, says 'e: 'Remember, I cawst you off. Don't come to me for nothin' after this. Don't ever you darken my doorstep ag'in,' 'e says. And Mr. Bayard, sir, 'e ups and laughs fiendish in 'is own father's fice. 'You've got another guess comin',' he mocks 'im open': 'you're in this business as deep as me,' 'e says, 'and if you cross me, I'll double-cross you, s'elp me Gawd, and in the newspapers, too.' And with that, out 'e went in a rige."

"So that was the way of it!" P. Sybarite commented dully.

So Mrs. Inche had sought the father to revenge herself upon the son; and with this outcome—Bayard unharmed, his father dead!...

"That was hexactly 'ow it 'appened, sir," affirmed the butler, rubbing his fat old hands.

"You 're wasting time. Go telephone the doctor," said P. Sybarite suddenly.

"Right you are, sir. But there's no real 'urry. He's dead as Guy Fawkes, and no doctor livin'—"

"Nevertheless, telephone—if you don't want to get into trouble."

"Quite right, sir. I'll do so at once."

Turning, the man waddled off, disappearing toward the back

of the house.

Alone, with neither hesitation nor a single backward glance at the body of his ancient enemy, the little man swung about, walked quietly to the front door, and as quietly let himself out.

He was of no mind to be called as a witness at a possible inquest; and business of far greater import urged him, the real business of his life, this: to discover the whereabouts of Marian Blessington with the least avoidable delay.

His first cast having failed, he must now try to draw the son; and, if possible, before the latter learned of his father's death.

Not until about to re-enter the car did he remember he had neglected to secure Bayard's address from the butler. But he wouldn't turn back; it could be ascertained elsewhere; Peter Kenny would either know it or know where to get it.

To Peter's rooms he must of necessity return first of all; for it would not much longer prove possible to go up and down and to and fro upon Manhattan Island in a black silk dress-coat and flaming scarlet small-clothes; to change was imperative.

"The Monastery," he directed, settling back into his seat.

It was now clear daylight: a morning of bright promise breaking over a Town much livelier than it had been half an hour or so ago, with more citizens abroad, some striding briskly to the day's work, some trudging wearily from the night's.

Over all brooded still that effect of illusion: this might have been, almost, a foreign city into whose streets he was adventuring for the first time, so changed and strange seemed everything in his eyes.

P. Sybarite himself felt old and worn and tired, and with a thoughtful finger rubbed an over-night growth of stubble upon his chin....

"Wait," he told the driver, on alighting at the Monastery; "I'm keeping you."

Money passed between them—more than enough to render his wishes inviolable.

A dull-eyed hallboy recognised and let him in, sullenly passing him on to the elevator; but as that last was on the point of taking flight to Peter Kenny's door, it hesitated; and the operator, with his hand on the half-closed gate, shot it open again instead of shut.

A Western Union messenger-boy, not over forty years tired, was being admitted at the street door. The colloquy there was distinctly audible:

"Mr. Bayard Shaynon?"

"Leventh floor. Hurry up—don't keep the elevator waitin'."

"Ah—ferget it!"

Whistling softly, the man with the yellow envelope ambled nonchalantly into the cage; fixed the operator with a truculent stare, and demanded the eleventh floor.

Now Peter Kenny's rooms were on the twelfth....

The telegram with its sprawling endorsement in ink, "*Mr. Bayard Shaynon, Monastery Apartments*," was for several moments within two feet of P. Sybarite's nose.

It was, indeed, anything but easy to keep from pouncing upon that wretched messenger, ravishing him of the envelope (which he was now employing artfully to split a whistle into two equal portions—and favour to none), and making off with it before the gate of the elevator could close.

Impossible to conjecture what intimate connection it might not have with the disappearance of Marian Blessington, what a flood of light it might not loose upon that dark intrigue!

Indeed, the speculations this circumstance set awhirl in P. Sybarite's weary head were so many and absorbing that he forgot altogether to be surprised or gratified by the favour of *Kismet* which had caused their paths to cross at precisely that instant, as if solely that he might be informed of Bayard Shaynon's abode....

"What door?" demanded Western Union as he left the cage at the eleventh floor.

"Right across the hall."

The gate clanged, the cage mounted to the next floor, and P. Sybarite got out, requiring no direction: for Peter Kenny's door was immediately above Bayard Shaynon's.

As he touched the bell-button for the benefit of the elevator man—but for his own, failed to press it home—the grumble of the door-bell below could be heard faintly through muffling fire-brick walls.

The grumble persisted long after the elevator had dropped back to the eleventh floor.

And presently the voice of Western Union was lifted in sour expostulation:

"Sa-ay, whatcha s'pose 's th' matta wid dis guy? I' been ringin' haffanour!"

"That's funny," commented the elevator boy: "he came in only about ten minutes ago."

"Yuh wuddn' think he cud pass away 's quick 's all that—wuddja?"

"Ah, I dunno. Mebbe he had a bun on when he come in. Gen'ly has. I didn' notice."

"Well, th' way he must be poundin' his ear now—notta hear dis racket—yud think he was trainin' for a Rip van Winkle Marathon."

Pause—made audible by the pertinacious bell, grinding away like a dentist's drill in a vacant tooth....

"Waitin' here all day won't get me nothin'. Here, what's th' matta wid you signin' for't?"

"G'wan. Sign it yourself 'nd stick unda the door, whydoncha?"

Second pause—the bell boring on, but more faintheartedly, as if doubting whether it ever would reach that nerve.

Finally Western Union gave it up.

"A'right. Guess I will."

Clang of the gate: whine of the descending car: silence....

Softly P. Sybarite tiptoed down the stairs.

Disappointment, however, lay in ambush for him at his nefarious goal: evidently Western Union had been punctilious about his duty; not even so much as the tip of a corner of yellow envelope peeped from under the door.

Reckless in exasperation, P. Sybarite first wasted time educing a series of short, sharp barks from the bell—a peculiarly irritating noise, calculated (one would think) to rouse the dead—then tried the door and, finding it fast, in the end knelt and bent an ear to the keyhole, listening....

Not a sound: silence of the grave; the house deathly still. He could hear his own heart drumming; but, from Shaynon's flat, nothing....

Or—was that the creak of a board beneath a stealthy footstep?

If so, it wasn't repeated....

Again, could it be possible his ears did actually detect a sound of human respiration through the keyhole? Was Bayard Shaynon just the other side of that inch-wide pressed-steel barrier, the fire-proof door, cowering in throes of some paralysing fright, afraid to answer the summons?...

If so, why? What did he fear? The police, perhaps? And if so— why? What crime had become his so to unman him that he dared not open and put his fate to the test?...

Quickly there took shape in the imagination of the little Irishman a hideous vision of mortal Fear, wild-eyed, white-lipped, and all a-tremble, skulking in panic only a little beyond his reach: a fancy that so worked upon his nerves that he himself seemed infected with its shuddering dread, and thought to feel the fine hairs a-crawl on his neck and scalp and his flesh a-creep.

When at length he rose and drew away it was with all stealth, as though he too moved in the shadow of awful terror bred of a nameless crime....

Once more at Peter Kenny's door, his diffident fingers evoked from the bell but a single chirp—a sound that would by no means have gained him admission had Peter not been sitting up in bed, reading to while away the ache of his wound.

But it was ordered so; Peter was quick to answer the door; and P. Sybarite, pulling himself together (now that he had audience critical of his demeanour) walked in with a very tolerable swagger—with a careless, good-humoured nod for his host and a quick look round the room to make certain they were alone.

"Doctor been?"

"Oh—an hour ago."

"And—?"

"Says I'm all right if blood-poisoning doesn't set in."

Shutting the door, Peter grinned not altogether happily. "That's one of the most fetching features of the new code of medical ethics, you know—complete confidence inspired in patient by utter frankness on doctor's part—and all that!...

"An insignificant puncture," he mimicked: "you'll be right as rain in a week—unless the wound decides to gangrene—it's apt to, all on its own, 'spite of anything we can do—in which case we'll have to amputate your body to prevent infection spreading to your head.'...

"Well?" he wound up almost gaily. "What luck?"

"The worst. Where are my rags? I've got to change and run. Also—while you're up"—Peter had just dropped into a chair—"you might be good enough to mix me a Scotch and soda."

Whereupon, while changing his clothes, and between breaths and gulps of whiskey-and-water, P. Sybarite delivered himself of an abbreviated summary of what had happened at the ball and after.

"But why," he wound up peevishly—"*why* didn't you tell me Bayard Shaynon lived in the flat below you?"

"Didn't occur to me; and if you ask me, I don't see why it should interest you now."

"Because," said P. Sybarite quietly, "I'm going down there and break in as soon as I'm dressed fit to go to jail."

"In the sacred name of Insanity—!"

"If he's out, I'll steal that telegram and find out whether it has any bearing on the case. If it hasn't, I'll sift every inch of the room for a suspicion of a leading clue."

"But if he's in—?"

"I'll take my chances," said P. Sybarite with grim brevity.

"Unarmed?"

"Not if I know the nature of the brute." He stood up, fully dressed but for his shoes. "Now—my gun, please."

"Top drawer of the buffet there. How are you going? Fire escape?"

"Where is it?" P. Sybarite asked as he possessed himself of his weapon.

"Half a minute." Peter Kenny held out his hand. "Let's have a look at that gun—will you?"

"What for?"

"One of those newfangled automatic pistols—isn't it? I've never seen one before."

"But—Great Scott!—you've had this here—"

"I know, but I didn't pay much attention—thinking of other things—"

"But you're delaying me—"

"Mean to," said Peter Kenny purposefully; and without giving P. Sybarite the least hint of his intention, suddenly imprisoned his wrist, grabbed the weapon by the barrel, and took it to himself—with the greater ease since the other neither understood nor attempted resistance.

"What in blazes—?" he enquired, puzzled, watching Peter turn the weapon over curiously in his hands. "I should think—"

"There!" Peter interrupted placidly, withdrawing the magazine clip from its slot in the butt and returning the now harmless mechanism. "Now run along. Fire-escape's outside the far window in the bedroom, yonder."

"What the deuce! What's the matter with you? Hand over that clip. What good is this gun without it?"

"For your present purpose, it's better than if loaded," Peter asserted complacently. "For purposes of intimidation—which is all you want of it—grand! And it can't go off by accident and make you an unintentional murderer."

P. Sybarite's jaw dropped and his eyes opened; but after an instant, he nodded in entire agreement.

"That's a head you have on your shoulders, boy!" said he. "As for mine, I've a notion that it has never really jelled."

He turned toward the bedroom, but paused.

"Only—why not say what you want? Why these roundabout ways to your purpose? Have you, by any chance, been educated for the bar?"

"That's the explanation," laughed Peter. "I'm to be admitted to practise next year. Meanwhile, circumlocution's my specialty."

"It is!" said P. Sybarite with conviction. "Well ... back in five minutes...."

Of all his weird adventures, this latest pleased him least. It's one thing to take chances under cover of night when your heart is light, your pockets heavy, and wine is buzzing wantonly within your head: but another thing altogether to burglarise your enemy's apartments via the fire-escape, in broad daylight, and cold-sober. For by now the light was clear and strong, in the open.

Yet to his relief he found no more than limpid twilight in the cramped and shadowed well down which zigzagged the fire-escape; while the opposite wall of the adjoining building ran blind from earth to roof; giving comfortable assurance that none could spy upon him save from the Monastery windows.

"One thing more"—Peter Kenny came to the window to advise, as P. Sybarite scrambled out upon the gridiron platform—"Shaynon's flat isn't arranged like mine. He's better off than I am, you know—can afford more elbow-room. I'm not sure, but I *think* you'll break in—if at all—by the dining-room window.... So long. Good luck!"

Clasping hands, they exchanged an anxious smile before P. Sybarite began his cautious descent.

Not that he found it difficult; the Monastery fire-escape was a series of steep flights of iron steps, instead of the primitive vertical ladder of round iron rungs in more general use. There was even a guard-rail at the outside of each flight. Consequently, P. Sybarite gained the eleventh floor platform very readily.

But there he held up a long instant, dashed to discover his task made facile rather than obstructed.

The window was wide open, to force whose latch he had thoughtfully provided himself with a fruit knife from Peter Kenny's buffet. Within was gloom and stillness absolute—the one rendered the more opaque by heavy velvet hangings, shutting out the light; the other with a quality individual and, as P. Sybarite took it, somehow intimidating—too complete in its promise.

And so for a darkly dubious moment the little man hung back. To his quick Celtic instinct there seemed to inhere, in that open, dark, and silent window, something as sinister and repellent as the inscrutable, soundless menace of a revolver presented to one's head.

Momentarily, indeed, he experienced anew something of that odd terror, unreasoning and inexcusable, that had assailed him some time since, outside the hall-door to this abode of enigmatic and uncanny quiet....

But at length, shaking his head impatiently—as if to rid it of its pestering swarm of fancies—he stepped noiselessly, in his unshod feet, down through the window, cautiously parted the draperies, and advanced into darkness so thick that there might as well have been night outside instead of glowing daybreak.

Then, with eyes becoming accustomed to the change, he made out shapes and masses that first confirmed Peter's surmise as to the nature of the room, and next gave him his bearings.

Over across from the window stood a door, its oblong dimly luminous with light softly shining down the walls of a private hall, from a point some distance to the left of the opening.

Rounding a dining-table, P. Sybarite stole softly on, and paused, listening, just within the threshold.

From some uncertain quarter—presumably the lighted room—he could hear a sound, very slight: so slight that it seemed guarded, but none the less unmistakable: the hiss of carbonated water squirting from a syphon into a glass.

Ceasing, a short wait followed and then a faint *"Aah!"* of satisfaction, with the thump of a glass set down upon some hard surface.

And at once, before P. Sybarite could by any means reconcile these noises with the summons at the front door that had been ignored within the quarter-hour, soft footfalls became audible in the private hall, shuffling toward the dining-room.

Instinctively the little man drew back (regretful now that he had yielded to Peter's prejudice against loaded pistols) retreating sideways along the wall until he had put the bulk of a massive buffet between him and the door; and, in the small space between that article of furniture and the corner of the room, waited with every nerve taut and muscle tense, in full anticipation of incontinent detection.

In line with these apprehensions, the footsteps came no further than the dining-room door; then died out for what seemed full two minutes—a pause as illegible to his understanding as their manifest stealth.

Why need Shaynon take such elaborate precautions against noises in his own lodgings?

Suddenly, and more confidently, the footfalls turned into the dining-room; and without glance right or left a man strode directly to the open window. There for an instant he delayed with an eye to the crack between the curtains; then, reassured, thrust one aside and stepped into the embrasure, there to linger with his head out of the window, intently reconnoitering, long enough to enable P. Sybarite to make an amazing discovery: the man was not Bayard Shaynon.

In silhouette against the light, his slight and supple form was unmistakable to one who had seen it before, even though his face was disfigured by a scant black visor across his eyes and the bridge of his nose.

He was Red November.

What P. Sybarite would have done had he been armed is problematical. What he did was remain moveless, even as he was breathless and powerless, but for his naked hands, either for offence or defence. For that November was armed was as unquestionable as his mastery of the long-barrelled revolver of blue steel (favoured by gunmen of the underworld) which he held at poise all the while he carefully surveyed his line of retreat.

At length, releasing the curtain, the gang leader hopped lightly out upon the grating, and disappeared.

In another breath P. Sybarite himself was at the window. A single glance through the curtains showed the grating untenanted; and boldly poking his head forth, he looked down to see the figure of the gunman, foreshortened unrecognisably, moving down the iron tangle already several flights below, singularly resembling a spider in some extraordinary web.

Incontinently, the little man ran back through the dining-room and down the private hall, abandoning every effort to avoid a noise.

No need now for caution, if his premonition wasn't worthless—if the vengeful spirit of Mrs. Inche had not stopped short of embroiling son with father, but had gone on to the end ominously shadowed forth by the appearance of the gunman in those rooms....

What he saw from the threshold of the lighted room was Bayard Shaynon still in death upon the floor, one temple shattered by a shot fired at close range from a revolver that lay with butt close to his right hand—carefully disposed with evident intent to indicate a case of suicide rather than of murder.

Louis Joseph Vance

XXI

THE SORTIE

At pains not to stir across the threshold, with quick glances P. Sybarite reviewed scrupulously the scene of November's crime.

Eventually his nod indicated a contemptuous conclusion: that it should not prove difficult to convict November on the evidence afforded by the condition of the apartment alone. A most superficial inspection ought to convince anybody, even one prone to precipitate conclusions, that Bayard Shaynon had never died by his own hand.

If November, in depositing the instrument of his crime close to the hand of its victim, had meant to mislead, to create an inference of *felo de se*, he had ordered all his other actions with a carelessness arguing one of three things: cynical indifference to the actual outcome of his false clue; sublime faith in the stupidity of the police; or a stupidity of his own as crass as that said to be characteristic of the average criminal in all ages.

The rooms, in short, had been most thoroughly if hastily ransacked—in search, P. Sybarite didn't for an instant doubt, of evidence as to the relations between Shaynon and Mrs. Inche calculated to prove incriminating at an inquest; though the little man entertained even less doubt that lust for loot had likewise been a potent motive influencing November.

He found proof enough of this in the turned-out pockets of

the murdered man; in the abstraction from the bosom of his shirt of pearl studs which P. Sybarite had noticed there within the hour; in the abraded knuckles of a finger from which a conspicuous solitaire diamond in massive antique setting was missing; in a pigskin bill-fold, empty, ripped, turned inside out, and thrown upon the floor not far from the corpse.

Then, too, in one corner stood a fine old mahogany desk of quaint design and many drawers and pigeonholes, one and all sacked, their contents turned out to litter the floor. In another corner, a curio cabinet had fared as ill. Even bookcases had not been overlooked, and stood with open doors and disordered shelves.

Not, however, with any notion of concerning himself with the assassin's apprehension and punishment did P. Sybarite waste that moment of hasty survey. His eyes were only keen and eager to descry the yellow Western Union message; and when he had looked everywhere else, his glance dropped to his feet and found it there—a torn and crumpled envelope with its enclosure flattened out and apart from it.

This last he snatched up, but the envelope he didn't touch, having been quick to remark the print upon it of a dirty thumb whose counterpart decorated the face of the message as well.

"And a hundred more of 'em, probably," P. Sybarite surmised as to the number of finger marks left by November: "enough to hang him ten times over ... which I hope and pray they don't before I finish with him!"

As for the dead man, he read his epitaph in a phrase, accompanied by a meaning nod toward the disfigured and insentient head.

"It was coming to you—and you got it," said P. Sybarite callously, with never a qualm of shame for the apathy with which he contemplated this second tragedy in the house of Shaynon.

Too much, too long, had he suffered at its hands....

With a shrug, he turned back to the hall door, listened an instant, gently opened it—with his handkerchief wrapped round the polished brass door-knob to guard against clues calculated to involve himself, whether as imputed principal or casual witness after the fact. For he felt no desire to report the crime to the police: let them find it out at their leisure, investigate and take what action they would; P. Sybarite had lost no love for the force that night, and meant to use it only at a pinch—as when, perchance, its services might promise to elicit the information presumably possessed by Red November in regard to the fate of Marian Blessington....

The public hall was empty, dim with the light of a single electric bulb, and still as the chamber of death that lay behind.

Never a shadow moved more silently or more swiftly than P. Sybarite, when he had closed the door, up the steps to Peter Kenny's rooms. Hardly a conceivable sound could be more circumspect than that which his knuckles drummed on the panels of Peter's door. And Peter earned a heartfelt, instant, and ungrudged blessing by opening without delay.

"Well?" he asked, when P. Sybarite—with a gesture enforcing temporary silence—had himself shut the door without making a sound. "Good Lord, man! You look as if you'd seen a ghost."

On the verge of agitated speech P. Sybarite checked to shake an aggrieved head.

"Bromides are grand for the nerves," he observed cuttingly, "but you're too young to need 'em—and I want none now.... Listen to me."

Briefly he told his story.

"Well, but the telegram?" Peter insisted. "Does it help—tell you anything? It's maddening—to think Marian may be in the power of that bloodthirsty—!"

"There you go again!" P. Sybarite complained—"and not two minutes ago I warned you about that habit. Wait: I've had time only to run an eye through this: let me get the sense of it."

Peter peering over his shoulder, the two conned the message in silence:

BAYARD SHAYNON
Monastery Apts., W. 43rd, N.Y.C.

Your wire received all preparations made send patient in charge as indicated at convenience legal formalities can wait as you suggest.

HAYNES PRIVATE SANATORIUM.

Blankly Peter Kenny looked at his cousin; with eyes in which deepening understanding mingled with anger as deep, and with profound misgivings as well, P. Sybarite returned his stare.

"It's as plain as the face on you, Peter Kenny. Why, all along I've had an indefinite notion that something of the sort was what they were brewing! Don't you see—'private sanatorium'? What more proof do you need of a plot to railroad Marian to a private institution for the insane? 'Legal formalities can wait as you suggest'—of course! They hadn't had time to cook up the necessary papers, to suborn medical certificates and purchase a commitment paper of some corrupt judge. But what of that?" P. Sybarite demanded, slapping the message furiously. "She was in the way—at large—liable at any time to do something that would put her money forever out of their reach. Therefore she must be put away at once, pending 'legal formalities' to ensure her permanent incarceration!"

"The dogs!" Peter Kenny growled.

"But consider how they've been served out—thunderbolts—justice from the very skies! All except one, and," said P. Sybarite solemnly, "God do so to me and more also if he's alive or outside bars before this sun sets!"

"Who?"

"November!"

"What can you do to him?"

"To begin with, beat him to that damned asylum. Fetch me the suburban telephone directory."

"Telephone directory?"

"Yes!" P. Sybarite raved. "What else? Where is it? And where are your wits?"

"Why, here—"

Turning, Peter took the designated volume from its hook beneath the wall instrument at the very elbow of P. Sybarite.

"I thought," he commented mildly, "you had all *your* wits about you and could see it."

"Don't be impudent," grumbled P. Sybarite, rapidly thumbing the pages. "Westchester," he muttered, adding: "Oscahana—H—Ha—H-a-d—"

"Are you dotty?"

"Look at that telegram. It's dated from Oscahana: that's somewhere in Westchester, if I'm not mistaken. Yes; here we are: H-a-y—Haynes Private Sanatorium—number, Oscahana one-nine. You call 'em."

"What shall I say?"

"Where the devil's that cartridge clip you took away from me?... Give it here.... And I want my money."

"But," Peter protested in a daze, handing over the clip and watching P. Sybarite rummage in the buffet drawer wherein he had banked his fortune before setting out for the Bizarre—"but what do you want me to—"

"Call up that sanatorium—find out if Marian has arrived. If she has, threaten fire and sword and—all that sort of thing—if they don't release her—hand her over to me on demand. If she hasn't, make 'em understand I'll dynamite the place if they let November bring her there and get away before I show up. Tell 'em to call in the police and pinch November on sight. And then get a lawyer and send him up there after me. And then—set the police after November—tell 'em you heard the shot and went down the fire-escape to investigate.... I'm off."

The door slammed on Peter as Bewilderment.

In the hall, savagely punching the elevator bell, P. Sybarite employed the first part of an enforced wait to return the clip of cartridges to its chamber in the butt of Mrs. Inche's pistol....

He punched the bell again....

He put his thumb upon the button and held it there....

From the bottom of the twelve-story well a faint, shrill tintinnabulation echoed up to him. But that was all. The car itself never stirred.

Infuriated, he left off that profitless employment and threw himself down the stairs, descending in great bounds from landing to landing, more like a tennis ball than a fairly intelligent specimen of mature humanity in control of his own actions.

Expecting to be met by the ascending car before halfway to the bottom, he came to the final flight not only breathless but in a towering rage—contemplating nothing less than a murderous assault as soon as he might be able to lay hands upon the hallboys—hoping to find them together that he might batter their heads one against the other.

But he gained the ground-floor lobby to find it as empty as his own astonishment—its doors wide to the cold air of dawn, its lights dimmed to the likeness of smouldering embers by the stark refulgence of day; but nowhere a sign of a hallboy or anything else in human guise.

As he paused to make sure of the reality of this phenomenon, and incidentally to regain his breath, there sounded from a distance down the street a noise the like of which he had never before heard: a noise resembling more than anything else the almost simultaneous detonations of something like half a dozen firecrackers of sub-cannon calibre.

Without understanding this or even being aware that he had willed his limbs to action, P. Sybarite found himself in the street.

At the curb his hired car waited, its motor purring sweetly but its chauffeur missing.

Subjectively he was aware that the sun was up and high enough to throw a sanguinary glare upon the upper stories of the row of garages across the street—those same from whose number he had chartered his touring car. And momentarily he surmised that perhaps the chauffeur had strolled over to the garage on some idle errand.

But no sooner had this thought enhanced his irritation than he had its refutation in the discovery of the chauffeur affection-ately embracing a lamp-post three or four doors away, toward Sixth Avenue; and so singular seemed this sight that P. Sybarite wondered if, by any chance, the fellow had found time to get drunk during so brief a wait.

At once, blind to all else, and goaded intolerably by his knowledge that the time was short if he were to forestall November at the asylum in Oscahana, he pelted hot-foot after the delinquent; came up with him in a trice; tapped him smartly on the shoulder.

"Here!" he cried indignantly—"what the deuce's the matter with you?"

The man showed him a face pale with excitement; recognised his employer; but made no offer to stir.

"Come!" P. Sybarite insisted irascibly. "I've no time to waste. Get a move on you, man!"

But as he spoke his accents were blotted out by a repetition of that portentous noise which had saluted him in the lobby of the Monastery, a moment since.

His eyes, veering inevitably toward the source of that uproar, found it quickly enough to see short, vicious jets of flame licking out against the gloom of an open garage doorway, nearly opposite the Hippodrome stage entrance—something like a hundred feet down the street.

"What," he cried, "in Hades—!"

"Gang fight," his chauffeur informed him briefly: "fly-cops cornered a bunch of 'em in November's garage—"

"*Whose* garage—?"

"Red November's! Guess you've heard of him," the man pursued eagerly. "That's right—he runs his own garage—taxis for Dutch House souses, yunno—"

"Wait!" P. Sybarite interrupted. "Let me get this straight."

Stimulated by this news, his wits comprehended the situation at a glance.

At the side of his chauffeur, he found himself in line with a number of that spontaneous class which at the first hint of sensation springs up from nowhere in the streets of Manhattan. Early as was the hour, they were already quite fifty strong; and every minute brought re-enforcements straggling up from Fifth Avenue.

But the lamp-post—still a mute, insensate recipient of the chauffeur's amorous clasp—marked a boundary beyond which curiosity failed to allure.

Similarly at Sixth Avenue, a rabble was collecting, blocking the roadway and backing up to the Elevated pillars and surface-car tracks—but to a man balking at an invisible line drawn from corner to corner.

Midway, the dark open doorway to November's garage yawned forbiddingly; and in all the space that separated these two gatherings of spectators, there were visible just three human figures: a uniformed patrolman, and two plain-clothes men—the former at a discreet distance, the two latter more boldly stationed and holding revolvers ready for instant employment.

"Fly-cops," the chauffeur named the two in citizen's clothing: "I piped 'em stickin' round while you was inside, an' was wonderin' what they was after, when all of a sudden I sees November duck up from the basement next door to the Monastery, and they tries to jump him. That ain't two minutes ago. November dodges, pulls a gun, and fights 'em off until he can back into the garage—"

A hand holding an automatic edged into sight round the corner of the garage door—and the pistol sang like a locust. Instantly one of the detectives fired. The pistol clattered to the walk as the hand disappeared. One shot at least had told for law and order.

"Anybody hurt yet?" P. Sybarite asked.

"Not that I know anythin' about."

"But what do you suppose makes 'em keep that door open? You'd think—"

"The way I figure it," the chauffeur cut in, "Red's plannin' to make his getaway in a car. He's just waitin' till the goin' looks good, and then he'll sail outa there like a streak of greased lightnin'. Yuh wanta be ready to duck, too, 'cause he'll come this way, an' keep guns goin' to prevent anybody from hinderin' him."

"Why this way? Sixth Avenue's nearer."

"Sure it is, but that way he'd have them L pillars to duck, to say nothin' of the crowd, and no tellin' but what a surface-car might block him. Yuh watch an' see 'f I ain't doped it out right."

From the dark interior of the besieged garage another automatic fluttered briskly; across the street a window fell in....

"Look here—you come with me," said P. Sybarite suddenly, plucking his chauffeur by the sleeve.

With a reluctant backward glance, the man suffered himself to be drawn apart from the crowd.

"How much nerve have you got?" the little Irishman demanded.

"Who—me? Why?"

"I want to stop this getaway—"

"Not for mine, friend." The chauffeur laughed scornfully. "I ain't lost no Red November!"

"Will a thousand dollars make you change your mind?"

The chauffeur's eyes narrowed.

"Whatcha drivin' at? Me—why—I'd take a lotta chances for a thousand."

"Help me—do as I say—and it's yours."

"Lead me to the coin," was the prompt decision.

"Here, then!"

P. Sybarite delved hastily into a trousers pocket and produced a handful of bills of large denominations.

"There's a five hundred dollar bill to start with," he rattled, stripping off the first that fell to his fingers—"and here's a hundred—no, here's another five instead."

"In the mitt," the chauffeur stipulated simply, extending his palm. "Either you're crazy or I am—but in the mitt, friend, and I'll run the car right into that garage, 'f you say so."

"Nothing so foolish as that." P. Sybarite handed over the two bills and put away the rest of his wealth. "Just jump into that car and be ready to swing across the street and block 'em as they come."

"You're on!" agreed the chauffeur with emotion—carefully putting his money away.

"And a thousand more"—his courage wrung this tribute from P. Sybarite's admiration—"if you're hurt—"

"You're on there, too—and don't think for a minute I'll letcha fergit, neither."

The chauffeur turned to his car, jumped into the driver's seat, and advanced the spark. The purr of the motor deepened to a leonine growl.

"Hello!" he exclaimed in surprise, real or feigned, to see P. Sybarite take the seat by his side. "What t'ell? Who's payin' *you* to be a God-forsaken ass?"

"Did you think I'd ask you to run a risk that frightened me?"

"Dunno's I thought much about it, but'f yuh wanta know what I think now, *I* think you oughta get a rebate outa whatcha give me—if you live to apply for it. And I don't mind tellin' you, if you do, you won't get it."

Again the spiteful drumming of the automatic: P. Sybarite swung round in time to see one of the plain-clothes men return the fire with several brisk shots, then abruptly drop his revolver, clap a hand to his bosom, wheel about-face, and fall prone.

A cry shrilled up from the bystanders, only to be drowned out by another, but fortunately more harmless, fusillade from the garage.

"Tunin' up!" commented the chauffeur grimly. "Sounds to me like they was about ready to commence!"

P. Sybarite shut his teeth on a nervous tremor and lost a shade or two of colour.

"Ready?" he said with difficulty.

The chauffeur's reply was muffled by another volley; on the echoes of which the little man saw the nose of a car poke diagonally out of the garage door, pause, swerve a trifle to the right, and pause once again....

"They're coming!" he cried wildly. "Stand by, quick!"

The alarm was taken up and repeated by two-score throats, while those dotting the street and sidewalks near by broke in swift panic and began madly to scuttle to shelter within doorways and down basement steps....

Like an arrow from the string, November's car broke cover at an angle. Ignoring the slanting way from threshold to gutter, it took the bump of the curb apparently at full tilt, and skidded to the northern curb before it could be brought under control and its course shaped eastward.

With a shiver P. Sybarite recognised that car.

It was not the taxicab that he had been led to expect, but the same maroon-coloured limousine into which he had assisted Marian Blessington at the Bizarre.

On its front seats were two men—Red November himself at the driver's side, a revolver in either hand. And the body of the car contained one passenger, at least, if P. Sybarite might trust to an impression gained in one hasty glance through the forward windows as the car bore down upon them— November's weapons spitting fire....

He could not say who that one passenger might be; but he could guess; and guessing, knew the automatic in his grasp to be useless; he dared not fire at the gangster for fear of loosing a wild bullet into the body of the car....

Now they were within fifty feet of one another. By contrast with the apparent slowness of the touring car to get in motion, the limousine seemed already to have attained locomotive speed.

A yell and a shot from one of November's revolvers (P. Sybarite saw the bullet score the asphalt not two feet from the forward wheel) warned them to clear the way as the gang leader's car swerved wide to pass them.

And on this the touring car seemed to get out of control, swinging across the street. Immediately the other, crowded to the gutter, attempted to take the curb, but, the wheels meeting it at an angle not sufficiently acute, the manoeuvre failed. To a chorus of yells November's driver shut down the brakes not a thought too soon—not soon enough, indeed, to avoid a collision that crumpled a mudguard as though it had been a thing of pasteboard.

Simultaneously P. Sybarite's chauffeur set the brakes, and with the agility of a hounded rabbit seeking its burrow, dived from his seat to the side of the car farthest from the gangsters.

In an instant he was underneath it.

P. Sybarite, on the other hand, had leaped before the accident.

Staggering a pace or two—and all the time under fire—he at length found his feet not six feet from the limousine. It had stopped broadside on. In this position he commanded the front seats without great danger of sending a shot through the body.

His weapon rose mechanically and quite deliberately he took aim—making assurance doubly sure throughout what seemed an age made sibilant by the singing past his head of the infuriated gangster's bullets.

But his finger never tightened upon the trigger.

November had ceased firing and was plucking nervously at the slide of his automatic. His driver had jumped down from his seat and was scuttling madly up the street.

In a breath P. Sybarite realised what was the matter: as automatics will, when hot with fast firing, November's had choked on an empty shell.

With a sob of excitement the little man lowered his weapon

and flung himself upon the gang leader.

November rose to meet him, reversing his pistol and aiming at
P. Sybarite's head a murderous blow. This, however, the little
man was alert to dodge. November came bodily into his arms.
Grappling, the two reeled and went down, P. Sybarite's fingers
closing on the throat of the assassin just as the latter's head
struck the pavement with brutal force.

The man shivered, grunted, and lay still.

P. Sybarite disengaged and got up on his feet.

XXII

TOGETHER

In a daze, P. Sybarite shook and felt himself all over, unable to credit his escape from that rain of bullets.

But he was apparently unharmed.

Kismet!...

Then suddenly he quickened to the circumstances: the thing was finished, November stunned and helpless at his feet, November's driver making off, the crowd swarming round, the police an imminent menace.

Now if Marian were in the body of the town-car, as he believed, he must get her out of it and away before the police and detectives could overtake and apprehend them both.

Instant action, inspired audacity, a little luck—and the thing might possibly be accomplished.

His chauffeur was crawling ignominiously out from beneath the touring car—his countenance livid with grime and the pallor of fright. Meeting the eye of his employer, he grinned a sheepish grin.

P. Sybarite seized him by the arm.

Louis Joseph Vance

"Are you hurt?"

"Not ten cents' worth—much less a thousand dollars! No such luck!"

His mouth to the fellow's ear, P. Sybarite whispered hoarsely and hurriedly:

"Unhook your license number—throw it in the car—get ready to move on the word—lady in that car—kidnapped—I love her—d'you understand?—we must get her away—another thousand in this for you—"

"Gotcha," the man cut in smartly. "And I'm with you to the last act! Go to it, bo'—I like your style!"

Swinging about, P. Sybarite jumped upon the running-board of the maroon-coloured car, wrenched the door open, and stumbled in.

In her evening frock and her cloak of furs, Marian lay huddled in a corner, wrists and ankles alike made fast with heavy twine, her mouth closed tight by a bandanna handkerchief passed round her jaws and knotted at the nape of her neck. Above its folds her face was like snow, but the little man thought to detect in her staring eyes a hint of intelligence, and on this he counted with all his soul.

"Don't scream!" he pleaded as, whipping out a pocket knife, he severed her bonds. "Don't do anything but depend on me. Pretend, if you like, you don't know what's happening—likely you don't at that! No matter. Have faith in me; I'll get you clear of this yet!"

He fancied a softening look in those wide and frightened eyes of a child.

An instant's work loosed her scored and excoriated wrists; in another, the bonds fell from her ankles. Deftly unknotting the bandage that closed her mouth, he asked could she walk. With difficulty, in a husky and painful whisper, but still courageously, she told him yes.

Hopeful, rather than counting on this assurance, he jumped out and offered his hand. She put hers into it (and it was cold as ice), stirred, rose stiffly, tottered to the door, and fell into his arms....

A uniformed patrolman, breaking through the crowd about them, seized P. Sybarite and held him fast.

"What's this? Who's this?" he gabbled incoherently, brandishing a vaguely formidable fist.

"A lady, you fool!" P. Sybarite snapped. "Let go and catch that scoundrel over there—if you're worth your salt."

He waved his free hand broadly in the direction taken by November's driver.

Abruptly and without protest the patrolman released him, butted his way through the crowd, and disappeared.

An arm boldly about Marian's waist, P. Sybarite helped her to the step of the touring car—and blessed that prince among chauffeurs, who was up and ready in his seat!

But now again he must be hindered: a plain-clothes man dropped a heavy hand upon his shoulder and screwed the muzzle of a revolver into P. Sybarite's ear.

"Under arrest!" he blatted wildly. "Carrying fire-arms! Causing a crowd to collect—!"

"All right—all right!" P. Sybarite told him roughly. "I admit it. I'm not resisting, am I? Take that gun out of my ear and help me get this lady into the car before she's trampled and torn to pieces by these staring fools!"

Stupidly enough, the man comprehended some part of his admonishment. Staring blankly from the little man to the girl, he pocketed his weapon and, grasping Marian's arm, assisted her into the touring car.

"Thanks!" cried P. Sybarite, jumping up on the running-board. "You're most amiable, my friend!"

And with the heel of his open hand he struck the man forcibly upon the chest, so that he reeled back, tripped over the hapchance foot of an innocent by-stander, and went sprawling and blaspheming upon his back.

Somebody laughed hysterically.

"Go!" P. Sybarite cried to the chauffeur.

The crowd gave way before the lunge of the car....

They were halfway to Fifth Avenue before pursuit was thought of; had turned the corner before it was fairly started; in five minutes had thrown it off entirely and were running free at a moderate pace up Broadway just above Columbus Circle....

"Where to now, boss?" the chauffeur presently enquired.

P. Sybarite looked enquiringly at his charge. Since her rescue she had neither moved nor spoken—had rested motionless in her corner of the tonneau, eyes closed, body relaxed and listless. But now she roused; unveiled the dear wonder of her eyes of brown; even mustered up the ghost of a smile.

"Wherever you think best," she told him gently.

"The Plaza? You might be bothered there. We may be traced—we're sure to. This only saves us for the day. To-morrow—reporters—all that—perhaps. Perhaps not!... Don't you know somebody out of town to whom you could go for the day? Once across the city line, we're safe for a little."

She nodded: breathed an address in Westchester County....

Some time later P. Sybarite became sensible of an amazing fact. A hand of his rested on the cushioned seat, and in it lay, now warm and wonderfully soft and light, Marian's hand.

He stared incredulously until he had confirmed the substance of this impression; looked up blinking; met the confident, straightforward, and wistful regard of the girl; and blushed to his brows.

The car swept on and on, through the golden hush of that glorious Sunday morning....

Louis Joseph Vance

XXIII

PERCEVAL UNASHAMED

Toward ten of that same Sunday morning a touring car of majestic mien drew up in front of a boarding-house in Thirty-eighth Street West.

From this alighted a little man of somewhat bedraggled appearance, wearing a somewhat weather-beaten but heartfelt grin.

Ostentatiously (or so it seemed to one solitary and sour-mouthed spectator, disturbed in his perusal of a comic supplement on the brownstone stoop of the boarding-house) he shook hands with the chauffeur, and, speaking guardedly, confirmed some private understanding with him.

Then the car rolled off, and P. Sybarite shuffled meekly in through the gate, crossed the dooryard, and met the outraged glare of George Bross with an apologetic smile and the request:

"If you've got a pack of Sweets about you, George, I can use one in my business."

Without abating his manifestation of entire disapproval, George produced a box of cigarettes, permitted P. Sybarite to select one, and helped himself.

They shared a match, even as brothers might, before honest

indignation escaped the grim portals of the shipping clerk's mouth.

"Sa-ay!" he exploded—"looky here: where've you been all night?"

"Ah-h!" P. Sybarite sighed provokingly: "that's a long and tiresome story, George."

With much the air of a transient, he sat him down by George's side.

"A very long and very weary story, George. I don't like to tell it to you, really. We'd be sure to quarrel."

"Why?" George demanded aggressively.

"Because you wouldn't believe me. I don't quite believe it myself, now that all's over, barring a page or two. Your great trouble, George, is that you have no imagination."

"The devil I ain't!"

"Perfectly right: you haven't. If you point with pride to that wild flight of fancy which identified 'Molly Lessing' with Marian Blessington, George, your position is (as you yourself would say) untenable. It wasn't imagination: it was fact."

"No!" George ejaculated. "Is that right? What'd I tell you?"

"Word of honour! But it's a secret, as yet—from everybody except you and Violet; and even you we wouldn't tell had you not earned the right to know by guessing and making me semi-credulous—enough to start something—several some-things, in fact."

"G'wan!" George coaxed. "Feed it to me: I'll eat it right outa your hand. Whatcha been doin' with yourself all night, P.S.?"

"I've been Day of Days-ing myself, George."

"Ah, can the kiddin', P.S. Come through! Whadja do?"

"Broke every Commandment in the Decalogue, George, barring one or two of the more indelicate ones; kicked the laws of chance and probability into a cocked hat; fractured most of the Municipal Ordinances—and—let me see—oh, yes!—dislocated the Long Arm of Coincidence so badly that all of its subsequent performances are going to seem stiff and lacking in that air of spontaneity without which—"

"My Gawd!" George despaired—"he's off again on that hardy annual talkalogue of his!... Lis'n, P.S.—"

"Call me Perceval," P. Sybarite suggested pleasantly.

"*Wh-at!*"

"Let it be Perceval hereafter, George—always. I grant you free permission."

"But I thought you said—"

"So I did—a few hours ago. Now I—well, I rather like it. It makes all the difference who calls you that sort of name first, and what her voice is like."

"One of us," George protested with profound conviction, "is plumb loony in the head!"

"It's me," said P. Sybarite humbly: "I admit it.... And the worst of it is—I like it! So would you if you'd been through a Day of Days."

George let that pass; for the moment he was otherwise engaged in vain speculation as to the appearance of a phenomenon rather rare in the calendar of that West Thirty-eighth Street boarding-house.

A Western Union boy, weary with the weariness of not less than forty summers, was shuffling in at the gate.

"Sa-ay!" he called with the asperity of ingrained ennui—"either of youse guys know a guy named Perceval Sybarite 't lives here?"

Silently P. Sybarite held out his hand, took the greasy little book in its black oil-cloth binding, scrawled his signature in the proper blank, and received the message in its sealed yellow envelope.

"Wait," he commanded calmly, eyeing Western Union with suspicion.

"W'at's eatin' you? Is they an answer?"

"They ain't no answer," P. Sybarite admitted.

"Well, whatcha want? I got no time to stick round here kiddin'."

"One moment of your valuable time. I believe you delivered a message at the Monastery Apartments in Forty-third Street this morning."

"Well, an' what 'f I did?"

"Only this."

P. Sybarite extracted an immense roll of bills from his pocket; transferred it to his other hand; delved deeper; eventually produced a single twenty-dollar gold-piece.

"Take this," he said, tossing it to the boy with princely nonchalance. "It's the last of a lot, but—it's yours."

"What for?" Western Union demanded in amaze; while, as for George Bross, *he* developed plain symptoms of apoplexy.

"You'll never know," said P. Sybarite. "Now run along before I come to."

In the shadow of this threat, Western Union fled precipitately....

P. Sybarite rose; yawned; smiled benignantly upon George Bross.

"I'm off to bed—was only waiting for this message," he announced; "but before I go—tell me; how much money does Violet think you ought to be earning before you're eligible for the Matrimonial Stakes?"

"She said somethin' oncet about fifty per," George remembered gloomily.

"It's yours—doubled," P. Sybarite told him. "To-morrow you will resign from the employ of Whigham & Wimper and go to Blessington's to enter their shipping department at a hundred a week; and if you don't earn it, may God have mercy on your wretched soul!"

George got up very suddenly.

"I'll go send for the doctor," he announced.

"One moment more." P. Sybarite dropped a detaining hand upon his arm. "You and Violet are invited to dinner to-night—at the Hotel Plaza. Don't be alarmed; you needn't dress; we'll dine privately in Marian's apartment."

"Marian!"

"Miss Blessington—Molly Lessing that was."

"Honest!" said George sincerely. "I don't know whether to think you've gone bughouse or not. You've always been a bit queer and foolish in the bean, but never since I've known you—"

"And after dinner," P. Sybarite pursued evenly, "you're going to attend a very quiet little wedding party."

"Whose, for God's sake?"

"Marian's and mine; and the only reason why you can't be best man is that the best man will be my cousin, Peter Kenny."

"Is that straight?"

"On the level."

George concluded that there was sanity in P. Sybarite's eyes.

"Well, I certainly got to slip you the congrats!" he protested. "And say—you goin' to bounce Whigham and Wimper, too?"

"Yes."

"And whatcha goin' do then?"

"I? To tell you the truth, I'm considering joining the Union and agitating for an eight-hour Day of Days. This one of mine has been eighteen hours long, more or less—since I got those theatre tickets, you know—and I'm too dog-tired to keep my eyes open another minute. After I've had a nap, I'll tell you all about everything." ...

But he wasn't too tired to read his telegram, when he found himself again, and for the last time, in his hall bedroom.

It said simply: "I love you.—Marian."

From this P. Sybarite looked up to his reflection in the glass. And presently he smiled sheepishly, and blinked.

"Perceval...!" murmured the little man fondly.

Choose from Thousands of 1stWorldLibrary Classics By

A. M. Barnard
Ada Leverson
Adolphus William Ward
Aesop
Agatha Christie
Alexander Aaronsohn
Alexander Kielland
Alexandre Dumas
Alfred Gatty
Alfred Ollivant
Alice Duer Miller
Alice Turner Curtis
Alice Dunbar
Allen Chapman
Ambrose Bierce
Amelia E. Barr
Amory H. Bradford
Andrew Lang
Andrew McFarland Davis
Andy Adams
Anna Alice Chapin
Anna Sewell
Annie Besant
Annie Hamilton Donnell
Annie Payson Call
Annie Roe Carr
Annonaymous
Anton Chekhov
Arnold Bennett
Arthur Conan Doyle
Arthur M. Winfield
Arthur Ransome
Arthur Schnitzler
Atticus
B.H. Baden-Powell
B. M. Bower
B. C. Chatterjee
Baroness Emmuska Orczy
Baroness Orczy
Basil King
Bayard Taylor
Ben Macomber
Bertha Muzzy Bower
Bjornstjerne Bjornson
Booth Tarkington
Boyd Cable
Bram Stoker
C. Collodi
C. E. Orr

C. M. Ingleby
Carolyn Wells
Catherine Parr Traill
Charles A. Eastman
Charles Amory Beach
Charles Dickens
Charles Dudley Warner
Charles Farrar Browne
Charles Ives
Charles Kingsley
Chàrles Klein
Charles Hanson Towne
Charles Lathrop Pack
Charles Romyn Dake
Charles Whibley
Charles Willing Beale
Charlotte M. Braeme
Charlotte M. Yonge
Charlotte Perkins Stetson
Clair W. Hayes
Clarence Day Jr.
Clarence E. Mulford
Clemence Housman
Confucius
Coningsby Dawson
Cornelis DeWitt Wilcox
Cyril Burleigh
D. H. Lawrence
Daniel Defoe
David Garnett
Dinah Craik
Don Carlos Janes
Donald Keyhoe
Dorothy Kilner
Dougan Clark
Douglas Fairbanks
E. Nesbit
E.P.Roe
E. Phillips Oppenheim
Earl Barnes
Edgar Rice Burroughs
Edith Van Dyne
Edith Wharton
Edward Everett Hale
Edward J. O'Biren
Edward S. Ellis
Edwin L. Arnold
Eleanor Atkins
Eliot Gregory

Elizabeth Gaskell
Elizabeth McCracken
Elizabeth Von Arnim
Ellem Key
Emerson Hough
Emilie F. Carlen
Emily Dickinson
Enid Bagnold
Enilor Macartney Lane
Erasmus W. Jones
Ernie Howard Pie
Ethel May Dell
Ethel Turner
Ethel Watts Mumford
Eugenie Foa
Eugene Wood
Eustace Hale Ball
Evelyn Everett-green
Everard Cotes
F. H. Cheley
F. J. Cross
F. Marion Crawford
Federick Austin Ogg
Ferdinand Ossendowski
Francis Bacon
Francis Darwin
Frances Hodgson Burnett
Frances Parkinson Keyes
Frank Gee Patchin
Frank Harris
Frank Jewett Mather
Frank L. Packard
Frank V. Webster
Frederic Stewart Isham
Frederick Trevor Hill
Frederick Winslow Taylor
Friedrich Kerst
Friedrich Nietzsche
Fyodor Dostoyevsky
G.A. Henty
G.K. Chesterton
Gabrielle E. Jackson
Garrett P. Serviss
Gaston Leroux
George A. Warren
George Ade
Geroge Bernard Shaw
George Durston
George Ebers

George Eliot
George Gissing
George MacDonald
George Meredith
George Orwell
George Sylvester Viereck
George Tucker
George W. Cable
George Wharton James
Gertrude Atherton
Gordon Casserly
Grace E. King
Grace Gallatin
Grace Greenwood
Grant Allen
Guillermo A. Sherwell
Gulielma Zollinger
Gustav Flaubert
H. A. Cody
H. B. Irving
H.C. Bailey
H. G. Wells
H. H. Munro
H. Irving Hancock
H. Rider Haggard
H. W. C. Davis
Haldeman Julius
Hall Caine
Hamilton Wright Mabie
Hans Christian Andersen
Harold Avery
Harold McGrath
Harriet Beecher Stowe
Harry Castlemon
Harry Coghill
Harry Houidini
Hayden Carruth
Helent Hunt Jackson
Helen Nicolay
Hendrik Conscience
Hendy David Thoreau
Henri Barbusse
Henrik Ibsen
Henry Adams
Henry Ford
Henry Frost
Henry James
Henry Jones Ford
Henry Seton Merriman
Henry W Longfellow
Herbert A. Giles

Herbert Carter
Herbert N. Casson
Herman Hesse
Hildegard G. Frey
Homer
Honore De Balzac
Horace B. Day
Horace Walpole
Horatio Alger Jr.
Howard Pyle
Howard R. Garis
Hugh Lofting
Hugh Walpole
Humphry Ward
Ian Maclaren
Inez Haynes Gillmore
Irving Bacheller
Isabel Hornibrook
Israel Abrahams
Ivan Turgenev
J.G.Austin
J. Henri Fabre
J. M. Barrie
J. Macdonald Oxley
J. S. Fletcher
J. S. Knowles
J. Storer Clouston
Jack London
Jacob Abbott
James Allen
James Andrews
James Baldwin
James Branch Cabell
James DeMille
James Joyce
James Lane Allen
James Lane Allen
James Oliver Curwood
James Oppenheim
James Otis
James R. Driscoll
Jane Austen
Jane L. Stewart
Janet Aldridge
Jens Peter Jacobsen
Jerome K. Jerome
John Burroughs
John Cournos
John F. Kennedy
John Gay
John Glasworthy

John Habberton
John Joy Bell
John Kendrick Bangs
John Milton
John Philip Sousa
Jonas Lauritz Idemil Lie
Jonathan Swift
Joseph A. Altsheler
Joseph Carey
Joseph Conrad
Joseph E. Badger Jr
Joseph Hergesheimer
Joseph Jacobs
Jules Vernes
Julian Hawthrone
Julie A Lippmann
Justin Huntly McCarthy
Kakuzo Okakura
Kenneth Grahame
Kenneth McGaffey
Kate Langley Bosher
Kate Langley Bosher
Katherine Cecil Thurston
Katherine Stokes
L. A. Abbot
L. T. Meade
L. Frank Baum
Latta Griswold
Laura Dent Crane
Laura Lee Hope
Laurence Housman
Lawrence Beasley
Leo Tolstoy
Leonid Andreyev
Lewis Carroll
Lewis Sperry Chafer
Lilian Bell
Lloyd Osbourne
Louis Hughes
Louis Tracy
Louisa May Alcott
Lucy Fitch Perkins
Lucy Maud Montgomery
Luther Benson
Lydia Miller Middleton
Lyndon Orr
M. Corvus
M. H. Adams
Margaret E. Sangster
Margret Howth
Margaret Vandercook

Margret Penrose
Maria Edgeworth
Maria Thompson Daviess
Mariano Azuela
Marion Polk Angellotti
Mark Overton
Mark Twain
Mary Austin
Mary Catherine Crowley
Mary Cole
Mary Hastings Bradley
Mary Roberts Rinehart
Mary Rowlandson
M. Wollstonecraft Shelley
Maud Lindsay
Max Beerbohm
Myra Kelly
Nathaniel Hawthrone
Nicolo Machiavelli
O. F. Walton
Oscar Wilde
Owen Johnson
P.G. Wodehouse
Paul and Mabel Thorne
Paul G. Tomlinson
Paul Severing
Percy Brebner
Peter B. Kyne
Plato
R. Derby Holmes
R. L. Stevenson
R. S. Ball
Rabindranath Tagore
Rahul Alvares
Ralph Bonehill
Ralph Henry Barbour
Ralph Victor
Ralph Waldo Emmerson
Rene Descartes
Rex Beach
Rex E. Beach
Richard Harding Davis
Richard Jefferies
Richard Le Gallienne
Robert Barr
Robert Frost
Robert Gordon Anderson
Robert L. Drake
Robert Lansing
Robert Lynd
Robert Michael Ballantyne

Robert W. Chambers
Rosa Nouchette Carey
Rudyard Kipling
Samuel B. Allison
Samuel Hopkins Adams
Sarah Bernhardt
Sarah C. Hallowell
Selma Lagerlof
Sherwood Anderson
Sigmund Freud
Standish O'Grady
Stanley Weyman
Stella Benson
Stella M. Francis
Stephen Crane
Stewart Edward White
Stijn Streuvels
Swami Abhedananda
Swami Parmananda
T. S. Ackland
T. S. Arthur
The Princess Der Ling
Thomas A. Janvier
Thomas A Kempis
Thomas Anderton
Thomas Bailey Aldrich
Thomas Bulfinch
Thomas De Quincey
Thomas Dixon
Thomas H. Huxley
Thomas Hardy
Thomas More
Thornton W. Burgess
U. S. Grant
Valentine Williams
Various Authors
Vaughan Kester
Victor Appleton
Victoria Cross
Virginia Woolf
Wadsworth Camp
Walter Camp
Walter Scott
Washington Irving
Wilbur Lawton
Wilkie Collins
Willa Cather
Willard F. Baker
William Dean Howells
William le Queux
W. Makepeace Thackeray

William W. Walter
William Shakespeare
Winston Churchill
Yei Theodora Ozaki
Yogi Ramacharaka
Young E. Allison
Zane Grey